all that's golden doesn't glitter

All that's golden doesn't glitter

Gaye Lynn Davis

Bookcraft

SALT LAKE CITY, UTAH

Library of Congress Catalog Card Number: 84-70563
ISBN 0-88494-528-6

First Printing, 1984

Lithographed in the United States of America
PUBLISHERS PRESS
Salt Lake City, Utah

For every mother
who finds her role to be
not quite what she had expected

CONTENTS

ONE

WHATEVER HAPPENED TO THE "IN-BETWEEN"?

Dear Mother: Frankly, this being a wife and mother isn't exactly what I had envisioned! I've read all the books and articles, but there must be a page missing somewhere. There hasn't been a clue in any of the seminars and workshops (and I've raptly attended every one within a radius of 1,000 miles). So, what it boils down to is, Why didn't you tell me it would be like this?

"Hold it right there!" Pat cried emphatically. "That's *not* right!" She threw on the brakes and looked me squarely in the eye. Some people might call my friend Pat a conservative driver. To my own way of thinking, she could be trusted with a prize Bentley in the parking lot of a major mall where silver dollars were being given to everyone for each pound of their weight! Then why such an erratic response when she was normally so placid, so mellow?

We were discussing another one of "those articles" about kids that day. It was the kind that starts with a statement like, "One morning we took Hyrum by the hand and told him firmly and quietly that Heavenly Father wanted him to be obedient. . . ." And turning the page, it ends, ". . . and Hyrum governed himself henceforth and forever. He was ever cheerful, re-

1

sponsible, and grateful. As he left home to become a stake president, he wept and thanked us for everything we had done." Sigh.

"There's something missing, all right," she continued seriously, "and that is about eighty pages in between that tell how many retakes and failures it took before little Hyrum *really* learned the lessons." Somehow, we concluded, those "in-between" pages do always seem to be missing.

"Why is it that everyone seems so bent on seeing only perfection?" we wondered. It's like a kind of tunnel vision. Goals are fine, and the loftier the better—but sometimes it seems as if nothing short of perfection is within the realm of our consideration. This is particularly true for mothers. Anything less than "perfect" seems to indicate unworthiness. Just occasionally, it would be refreshing (to say the least) to hear about the "in-between": reality!

Pat and I agreed that we are all definitely the victims of "perfection overkill." It's tragic enough that we are constantly the targets of "professionals" (who know absolutely everything about everything, or is it nothing about nothing?). But in addition to their ever-growing rank and file, there's the small (but never silent) number of "perfect mothers." They're the ones with "perfect" husbands and "perfect" children (particularly the latter). They are the ones with the never-ending lists of ways *they* say we can all achieve the "perfect" home.

It just can't be that simple, we think. And guess what? It isn't! This becoming perfect definitely is not as easy as they make it out to be, but it might not really be that complicated, either. Could it be that we can push ourselves steadily toward that ultimate ideal, even while caught in our reality? Could that goal be better achieved if we were to focus our attention not so much on the goal itself as on the "in-betweens" that lead toward it? Facing them. Accepting them. Dealing with them. Using them. Isn't this, after all, our challenge in life? (Ah-hah! The smoke is beginning to clear.)

There's hope.

TWO

DO I WHAT?

Dear Mom: Can you believe it? *Some moron I met at the Christmas party asked me if I* worked! *Me! The mother of a small tribe! What kind of a stupid question is that, anyway? My first impulses were (1) to fall down and die of laughter, or (2) to grab him by his lapels and hysterically rant: "Do I work? You bet I work—a lot harder than I ever did when I got paid for it!" But I resisted and chirped, "Who me? Work? Why no! I'm only a mother!"*

One of these days I'll see it advertised in the paper: Career Opportunity: Management position for talented, motivated woman; challenging opportunity, educational benefits, unlimited potential . . ." and know that it's aimed at me, the mother. But for now, the market is for secretaries, technicians, and market analysts. All these people "of the world" just don't seem to get the picture. Can they really think I don't work?

Actually, what they think doesn't matter, because *I* know motherhood is more than just work—it's my profession! What's more, I'm really happy in my work; it suits me to a T. Somewhat smug in that feeling I stop and then I remember. It wasn't always that way.

Most Latter-day Saint women inherit their career with marriage: a home career. For many it is the profession of their choice, and they couldn't be happier. For others it seems to be the one they get by default. No matter how we each view it individually, we know by the Spirit that the choice is the right one. Still, knowing that doesn't always make it easy.

Even for that girl who enters her home profession with rose-colored glasses and dreams of rainbows, the bubble will undoubtedly be burst by reality. She may become one of too many who come to see home as the place where they must "endure to the end." If such mothers could step out and look beyond the fog, they would see that there really are rainbows to be found.

When do we reach that point at which we realize that this is the place we want to be, despite it all? Perhaps the moment of revelation is in realizing that it takes time, not only for ourselves, but for anyone who begins a new profession.

Few people have instant happiness or success (very few, extremely few . . . are there really any?). Does a handsome, bright, young graduate walk into the doorway of his new profession, diploma still hot in his fist, and proclaim: "I just *knew* it! I knew I would love it! It's going to be a snap. Look out success, because here I come!" Probably not. His learning period and a lot of just plain hard work are ahead. He may grow to love his work and have success, but that comes only in time, and there's a price to pay.

We (mothers, homemakers, housewives, whatever we prefer to call ourselves—the title is really unimportant), we too have to learn the work of our profession before there will be any real dividends. And even though home is our profession, it also is just plain hard work. However, in our somewhat generalized profession there isn't a pay scale tied to the cost-of-living index, and success doesn't come merely through seniority.

"Just hanging on" won't get us very far. Look at that graduate again. If he acts bored, lackadaisical, trapped, or just "hangs on" waiting to get paid in the end (ever heard the saying, "You'll get

4

your blessings in heaven''?), what happens? He will not only become disenchanted and dissatisfied, but he probably won't even get paid for long.

"But that's the real world," cries Hedy Housewife. "It isn't even comparable." Isn't it? Hedy needs to come to a screeching halt and realize that there's no world more "real" than that of the wife and mother.

If there were a best-seller list for the subconscious mind, *The Power of Intimidation* would rank number one. Intimidation may be subtle or blatant, but it is always powerful. And where is it aimed? At *us!* Women are among Satan's most hammered targets at this point in the dispensations. He knows how close the Lord's coming is (even if we don't). And he thrusts his energies now in the direction where the most damage can be done to hamper our Father's plan—in the home. (And who remains the critical figure in that home? Yes, you, the woman.) Satan knows us, unfortunately, and also what means to best employ against our effectiveness in that critical place.

The world (really a euphemism for the father of lies) is making too much of its mark on our Father's daughters. There are as many different methods as there is breadth of Satan's imagination. Consider how we are constantly reminded of things the world thinks we *can't* do; it chips away at many of us. (Our youth are particularly vulnerable.) Examples: A woman *can't* be fulfilled in the home. She *can't* contribute to society as a "housewife." She *can't* find meaning in life by having babies. She *can't* effectively raise those babies without degrees and worldly experiences. She *can't* be at all bright or grow intellectually at home. And, of course, a woman *can't* ever really be happy or fulfilled while trapped, squashed, and emotionally brutalized by a group of takers dubbed "the family." While not always the rule, it is still more than the exception to find this type of approach pointing out the endless ways that women who are "only mothers" *can't.*

And then we are pulled and enticed toward the glamour and allure supposedly found in a "real" career. Think about it: What is so fulfilling about waiting on tables, crawling in a mine shaft, punching keyboards, or auditing accounts? A means to an end, no doubt. But *fulfilling?*

Well, what about advocacy for women? *Advocacy* has carried such a negative connotation that Latter-day Saints (both men and women) often look at it as being a negative thing. I hope that's not true in reality—because I am definitely a woman's advocate. Every woman should be a woman's advocate. For even though we recognize inequalities and inadequacies that affect lives to the point of tragedy, we should also be able to face the hard fact that equity and satisfaction will never come through worldly manipulations. They can come only through proper exercise of principles based on truth, principles of the gospel. Yes, in reality it is the Church that is the strongest, staunchest advocate for women to be found anywhere.

The world is long on promises, but it generally delivers nothing. On the one hand it promises professional glitter, on the other publishes loudly that home is where talents disappear, where personality smothers. But what does it deliver in actuality? Constraint, false security, entrapment—zero!

The world claims for the most part that in the home a vibrant personality will lose its sparkle and appetite for accomplishment, as if it were the job rather than the personality that determined the outcome. Satan really insults our intelligence with such a sham. A woman takes her own talents and interests into whatever profession she enters. It is not the job itself but the caliber of the person and what she makes of an opportunity that determine the outcome. Still, with enough repetition the drop, drop, drop wears at us.

Yes, the world is great with its claims. What we often forget, however—and what the world does not publish loudly at all—is that there are a great many bored and dissatisfied and depressed public accountants, attorneys, and retailers!

The allure of the professions in the competitive marketplace has been over exaggerated. It is becoming more apparent with the passage of time that many of the women who have left the home (either by choice or circumstance) are now viewing those of us at home as the ones to be envied. The sweet solitudes and opportunities of the home are missed more and more. It's no longer uncommon when answering the "Do you work?" question to hear in return, "Oh, how fortunate for you that you are able to stay home."

As long as we fence on Satan's ground it will never be easy for us. That means that if we are standing with our true footing in worldly philosophy and yet trying to ward off the blows as they come, eventually we will lose. We must foot ourselves firmly on the Lord's ground. In other words, we learn to choose the right, not just because it is right, but because that is what we *want.* We develop ourselves to the point that we not only *do* what the Lord would want, but we *want* what he would want. When we come to that point, then the vision opens widely before us. We see, we comprehend, and we embrace our callings. We then know that our designations as queens can only come through our homes, and we rejoice in that knowledge. But this does not come in the beginning.

Reams have been written about how we *should* feel and the way things *should* go. Meanwhile, some well-intentioned mother sits frustrated, wondering what is wrong with her. "Why isn't it working out? Is this all there is? Where's the reward?" she questions. We can each appreciate the predicament. But remember, rewards come only after the price has been paid. The amount of satisfaction we gain depends entirely on the amount of effort we put in.

A gumball doesn't pop out of the machine until a penny is put in *and* the handle is turned. It is futile to spend time moaning, "I'd really be a better wife *if . . .*" or, "I'd be a happier mother *if . . .*" What works is honest evaluation: Have I put in my "penny's worth" and also turned the handle?

In our exasperation, we cry, "There's so much to learn, so much to do!" That's true. And as we grow, we realize all the more what there is yet to do and to learn. But certainly we have enough fundamental faith to know that our Heavenly Father doesn't give us the opportunity and encourage us in that direction only to thwart us with obstacles that say, in effect, "You couldn't have had it anyway." He gives "commandments not a few" to "they that are faithful and diligent before me" (D&C 59:4). Every day, every challenge, takes us that much closer to success. We have the constant reminder: Within this seemingly insignificant little person are literally the elements of godhood. And that is really exciting. Remember, it isn't *only* today that counts, but *every* today.

So hang on. Don't give up. Success takes training. And effort isn't enough, either; success takes relentless effort. Sometimes we feel as though we are running a marathon—what pain! But this is the only road to success. We can't give up just because it seems that nothing we do works. We can't quit learning or experimenting. We can arrange and then rearrange our methods as our needs change. After all, we arrange and rearrange furniture, trying to find the very best way that "works," so why not our methods? I know that some men are convinced that the furniture has become worn out not by being sat on but by being shoved about. Sometimes our other efforts too may not seem as successful as we would wish, but the right combination is there somewhere.

We live in a society of "instants" from potatoes to shines on pianos. It is easy for us to grow impatient. But although success for us won't come instantly, the rewards will be—literally—heavenly.

THREE

Y-O-U SPELLS FOURTEEN KARAT

. . . Got a question for you, Mom. In Relief Society we heard we should go home, take a bubble bath by candlelight, and think beautiful thoughts. It was supposed to do wonders for us. So, thinking, What have I got to lose, I tried it. I went straight home, popped popcorn for the kids, unplugged the phone, and put all the "bathtime-should-be-a-beautiful-experience" equipment in the darkened bathroom. Then I shut and locked the door. After quietly sliding into the tub and pulling the curtain, I lit the candle. Ah, the prospect of solitude! Just as I settled down into a mountain of bubbles, the door flew open and the curtain tore back. There they stood—a host of naked little bodies—screeching in unison, "Can we get in with you, Mommy?" Mom, is it really worth it to try?

There was a popular song a few years go that eulogized "the everyday housewife who gave up the good life for me." That thinking, unfortunately, is accepted as fact by a great many women. Do we really have to give up "the good life" by being the "everyday housewife"? Is the girl inside gone forever? No more dreams, no thrill of life? The bottom line: Have we no choice? Do our external circumstances have to overpower the person within?

While in the Air Force my husband and I received orders transferring us to, of all places, *Alaska!* Sourdoughs and travel agents may call Alaska "The Last Frontier," but to my way of thinking what they meant was "The Twilight Zone." I felt that the earth would have to stop rotating long enough for us to step off into exile. And then the earth would continue—round and round until our tour of duty was over. Everything and everyone in the whole world except me would continue to grow and experience. There was no doubt in my mind that when the earth again allowed me to step on, the only growing I would have done would have been growing older!

What a surprise was in store! Our Alaska experience was truly a great one. The biggest shock of all, however, was my realization that Heavenly Father didn't want me to hibernate spiritually. The government had not actually plotted to incarcerate me mentally. My husband certainly had never intended that I should feel doomed emotionally. It was just circumstance. What I did with those particular circumstances would be up to me.

"I'll just *never* be able to do all the things I'm supposed to do to become perfect!" That must be one of the most common cries of despair from women in the Church. We could easily add: "I'm too worn out to really care about myself," or, "I can't do anything extra; I'd feel guilty when there are so many to care for and so much that we need," or, "I'm just not happy—I don't know why." The list could go on and on.

The classic comment, though, surely is this: "There's just not enough time for everything; how do you know what to leave out?" It could more correctly be asked, "How do you know whom to leave out?" And a real probability exists that the one who is left out is *you!* "For all the humiliation you suffer, for all the times you've saved the day, is it any wonder that only the best is good enough for you," says the smiling mommy on the television screen—talking to her dog! Why don't we consider ourselves worthy of at least the same amount of consideration?

Somehow we just don't seem to have any time for ourselves.

Many of us have large families that take an enormous amount of time and energy. We involve ourselves in endless activities in support of husband, church, children, community, and school. Couple that amount of activity with the attitude that we should be "anxiously engaged" trying to fulfill *every* commandment, suggestion, thought, and possibility *right now,* and we're stuck.

Truly there is a time and a season—for planting, growing, and then harvesting. It isn't possible to do everything for everyone every single time. Just as mechanical devices must have maintenance for efficiency, so must we. We know there will be no blessing if we do things at the expense of our families. But what we forget sometimes is that *we too* are a part of that family. The scriptures tell us there is a "time to every purpose under the heaven" (Ecclesiastes 3:1). The question is whether or not we are willing to pay the price to use that time properly.

It is sad to see many women—even young women—who seem to have no interest in themselves, or in life. They may be lethargic or apathetic, or perhaps they feel that the end results just don't justify the effort involved. This type of symptom may indicate an occupational hazard recognized in many professions as "burnout." "Burnout" strikes homemakers, too, but often with greater frequency and at an earlier age than it does those in other fields.

Simply translated, "burnout" means "no end in sight." The demands of wife, and particularly mother, are twenty-four hours a day, seven days a week, four weeks a month, and twelve months a year, year after year after year. She's always on call, the demand is constant, and rewards seem paltry at times.

In other professions those with "burnout" may choose either to find new employment or to strike. For mother, these are unreasonable and unsatisfactory cures. And so the condition may continue, growing worse with the passage of time. Unfortunately, there's no accompanying caution label to warn about the danger it may pose to her physical, emotional, and spiritual good health. Many know the pain, and some even recognize the need

11

for help. But for some elusive reason the majority seem to think it shows a lack of character, or indicates selfishness, or exposes weakness to admit the need to think of themselves.

Our lives are portioned out in what seem to be fifty different directions. But a woman's individuality is important, too. President Spencer W. Kimball reminded women that when sectioning our lives into pieces like a pie (each piece representing a block of time spent as a wife, a mother, a Church worker, a volunteer, and so forth) that somewhere there should be a piece representing the time that we spend taking care of *ourselves. Do not feel guilty about taking some time for yourself.* Do the very best you can for yourself. The classic phrase that sells so many millions of dollars worth of cosmetics—"I'm worth it!"—applies nowhere more than to you.

Taking Care of You—Physically

Early in our lives we learn not to take things at "face value." After all, we learn, "it's what's on the inside that really counts." That's true. Nevertheless, the way we look on the outside *does* make a remarkable difference in the way we feel about the inside. It certainly affects our efficiency level. Women all like to feel that they are the best they can be. We feel happier in our life situations if we feel good about the way we look. Having our hair done gives us a lift. When we're overweight, we get down in the dumps.

Our "face value" can work magic or havoc on those close to us, too. My husband almost went into shock that first Halloween party we went to after our marriage. I walked through the door wearing his old robe (vintage pioneer robe—came across the plains on an oxcart), a pair of old, furry slippers (also came across the plains—via gopher holes), with cold cream on my face, and dangling curlers. The accessory? A frying pan, of course. "Housewife. Get it?" I chortled. It was a riotous costume, I thought, but my husband did *not.* Later that evening I made a silent vow that I would never own an old robe or slippers and would never wear curlers anywhere. And he doesn't know it yet, but someone living in a little blue house in Anchorage will probably unearth that robe from the garden near the raspberries one day—because that's where I buried it.

You haven't stumbled upon the word *beautiful* here, and you won't. What's important is that individually, each of us is the best she can be. We live today in a "younger-the-better, thinner-the-better" thinking society. That has to be frustrating, for we're young only briefly, and most of us will gain some weight somewhere through the years. But just as "beautiful" isn't of any import, neither is "thin." "Thin" is valuable only in terms of practical value. By that I mean that it is important to the degree that it affects other areas of our lives, such as health or emotional stability. It's not only unreasonable, but foolish, for a forty-five-year-old woman to be dissatisfied because she hasn't retained the look of an eighteen-year-old girl.

However, if the truth must be known, it can be stated simply: Life is absolutely too short to be lived on a diet. It shouldn't be out of the realm of possibility to find a *realistic* weight at which one can feel good both physically and emotionally. That realistic weight for one thirty-year-old woman may not be even similar to that of her thirty-year-old friend.

Of course, there are periods of extenuating circumstances, such as the years of "Is she pregnant, or is she not?" The years of pregnancy and babies don't last forever (do they?), but if we don't work to keep the incentive alive, the extra weight we gain with each pregnancy *will* last forever.

Being startled into reality about the way we're taking care of ourselves may build the incentive we need. "Oh, do I sound *that* bad?" is almost always a person's first reaction when he hears a tape recording of his own voice. Our four-year-old son lovingly put his arms around me one day and sweetly purred, "I just love my *big* mommy." Out of the mouths of babes. . . . All right, the scales at home didn't exactly match the doctor's weight chart. (But then, everyone knows the weights listed on those charts are figured by a man!) All things considered, though, mirrors and children don't lie. When the time arrives that we find ourselves in sad shape (literally), then it's time for no more excuses.

And how inventive we are when it comes to excuses! Some things never change. As teenagers we used to write phony excuse letters for physical education classes. After all, jumping up and down a couple of times on a trampoline could ruin a hairstyle. But no one ever brought a note that read, "Mary is ill today." Instead they were always melodramatic situations: "Lawanna had trouble breathing during the night," or "Odie May's bone marrow has been bothering her lately." Was it any wonder that the teachers were able to isolate the few legitimate notes from the stacks of counterfeits?

That creative knack never leaves us. There are some legitimate reasons for our weak spots—but there certainly are more counterfeits! As to unwanted weight—legitimate: "I eat too much." Counterfeit: "Well, I really don't eat." (Ready? Here comes the rest of that line.) "I just clean up the kids' plates." Then there's this one: "I just can't stand to see anything go to waste." It's amazing that hubbard squash and black-eyed peas go down the disposal by the tons, but very seldom is a brownie or a piece of lemon chiffon pie lost to the trash can.

A point comes where we must be perfectly honest with ourselves. We must decide whether or not losing weight, for instance, is important. If we *do* want to trim down a little, then the things that can't be "recycled" can be tossed. Even if it does mean a little waste, not nearly as much will be lost in food as in self-esteem if we hang on to excuses that are so flimsy.

Many times the mother's interpretation of "waste not, want not" means "if they don't eat it, I have to." Not so. If visiting teachers bring fudge, make your children finish every last crumb while you sit on your hands, or immediately give it to the neighbors. (They'll think you're so sweet—two blessings for the price of one!) Is this approach drastic? Yes, but it's worth it if you're happy with yourself. There are fewer things that make a more dramatic change in a woman's self-esteem than losing some extra weight.

However, we are very wrong to carry this notion too far, either for ourselves or others. If being a few pounds overweight does not have an effect on the other areas of life, and a woman feels content and values herself, then why should she spend life on a diet just because the rest of the world seems compelled to do so? Self-esteem and health, not weight, are really the issues. And if we judge others by such a flimsy measure as how big or small they are, we are showing who the truly insecure person is.

Of one thing we are sure—our cosmetic appearance is completely irrelevant to the One who counts the most. To Him we are each cherished, valued, and priceless friends and individuals. As we mature, we learn to view ourselves that same way, regardless of what trends are being followed in our society. Then, we discover the ultimate in self-esteem.

But for the present, it seems that when we do the best *for* ourselves we feel the best *about* ourselves. Sometimes we may need a shot in the arm to climb back on the bandwagon. One cold, dark February our squadron wives had their monthly get-together. At the appointed hour, we all arrived bundled in parkas, mittens, hats, and clunky boots or furry mukluks. (They sound cute, but they are still clunky boots.) Frankly, the situation didn't offer much inspiration to look one's best. In the first place, our husbands were out of town as usual. And what does it matter what you wear to a meeting when "covered by cloak of night"? And who wants to wear anything more than "casual" with those boots? And why spend too much time on your hair when you'll probably keep your hat on the entire time anyway? And so forth and so on.

As we found our places all eyes were drawn again and again to the "new one." Whispers went back and forth, "Who is *she?*" She obviously had just arrived from the "Lower Forty-eight" because we hadn't seen anyone who looked or dressed like her since *we* had arrived. She was actually wearing heels. Surprise! She was our guest that dismal day and had come to make a presentation on the importance of personal appearance. That good-looking fellow with her was her—son! Everyone looked at her in utter disbelief, then we looked at each other, and then at our-selves. There have been fewer more captivated audiences. Was she beautiful? "Well-preserved"? No, merely conscientious.

Each woman has her own best side. How is it found? First, take a good, hard look at yourself in the mirror. Confront your-self in the morning after your shower (*au naturel*, of course). Is that "just a couple of extra pounds" really fifteen or twenty un-necessary ones? Then look again later in the day. Gracious, what on earth are you wearing? Your husband's socks? What reflection stares back before bed?

Why does it matter? Because what we do *counts*. We do not truly appreciate what an impact we have on those around us.

It's always seemed interesting that others invariably tend to classify all Latter-day Saints in the same category with the one Mormon they actually know. A friend mentioned she was inter-ested in having a nonmember neighbor attend a class she was teaching. That neighbor had lived for a time in Salt Lake City, but the only Latter-day Saint he had actually known personally had been a strapping, six-foot-tall man. And to him, all Mormons were the same. The teacher had hoped that by mingling in the pre-dominantly member group this neighbor would realize that there were in the Church real people—some fat, some thin, and many of whom laughed regularly. To that neighbor's way of thinking, "Mormon" was synonymous with "tall, stern, and disciplined." Although there are certainly worse traits by which to be known, there are also many other more positive possibilities.

When you hear, "I lived by a Mormon lady once," don't you hold your breath hoping that the next comment will be some-thing really positive: "She was the kindest . . ." or "What a sweet little mother!" or "What efficiency!" But at the same time there's a little fear the judgments will be less than kind: "Poor thing, trying to catch up to all those rowdy kids," or "Are all Mormon women so dowdy?" or "She surely did yell a lot, and that house!"

There's a real possibility that others will always tend to clas-sify and group us. Doesn't it make sense, then, that we should each take the responsibility personally to act as a public relations representative for the Church? *We* are The Church of Jesus Christ of Latter-day Saints as far as others are concerned.

A woman doesn't need a closetful of clothes to be her best, but she must be clean and neat. If it's got a hole in it, make it into a quilt top, mend it, or throw it away. Pretend there's a mirror on the front door and ask yourself how you look every time you leave the house for any reason whatsoever short of taking out a trash can. Is your hair clean and neat? Or does it look like it was cut with a knife and fork, or combed with a rake? These are hard things to face realistically, but everyone we meet views us with painful honesty. We have to view ourselves the same way if we ever hope to improve.

Time marches on. Unfortunately, many of us don't march with it, because we're still wearing clothes or have makeup and hairstyles that have long been out of style. It may be that keeping the same "look" helps us not to feel that passage of time. But there seems to be another side to the picture, too. For some curious reason many Latter-day Saint women think they should feel ashamed, or guilty, or extravagant if they are interested in maintaining any sense of style whatsoever. Why is that?

Just because we know the *inside* is more important, should we make it a point to neglect the *outside?* We are not necessarily slaves to fashion or "worldly" simply because we want to look the best we can. It's not a sign of vanity to buy something new occasionally for ourselves. It is not impossible, costly, or even difficult to be comfortably stylish and at the same time maintain a sense of modesty and appropriateness in our dress.

And, of course, taking care of the physical you means doing what is necessary for your good health. It should go without saying: get enough sleep, proper nutrition, and exercise in some way.

Your physical health is important because if there is sickness in one area, you will hurt somewhere else as well. Being in optimum shape will help give you confidence, enthusiasm, and that "I-can-handle-anything" attitude.

Taking Care of You—Mentally

"Help! I'm spending my entire lifetime in this kitchen!" We can each appreciate such a frustration. The demands of our lives are so many that it becomes painfully easy for us to wake up only to find ourselves buried—mentally. And no matter what or who the culprit is, buried is *buried.*

Our mental development is probably our easiest area to ignore. But in the pie piece of time for *you,* there have to be different bites. One bite is for the physical (just discussed). A second bite must be for your mental care. If all we care for is the physical body, the effect we desire can't be achieved, for we are much more than just bodies. And our lack of vision regarding our body's potential is *nothing* compared to the potential of our mind. It takes effort in the very best, and even dogged determination for others.

Have you ever commented (who hasn't?), "Wouldn't you just love to have a mind like that?" You do. Give yourself the credit you deserve! Our minds are almost always of greater capacity than we think. But we are modest, or perhaps insecure. Then there are those who offer never ending cop-outs, as if to justify their lack of ambition. For example, "Well, we can't all be scripturalists, can we?" Can't we? Why not? We can, if we're willing to pay the price.

Let's face it: Our minds are going to constantly absorb information anyway, for none of us live in a void. As to the selection of input, however, we are on our own. Do our circumstances rule or do we control them? Would we sift through a pile of garbage hoping for a chance morsel while a banquet is set within easy reach? It doesn't make sense. Worthwhile input does take effort, but it's neither difficult nor painful.

Does this mean "education"? Is this a suggestion that we put our families into debt, leave children in child-care centers, or ignore other responsibilities to go back to school? Absolutely not! It should be chiseled upon our foreheads: *"Education* is not the same as *degrees.* Formal education is a magnificent opportunity that should be taken advantage of when the opportunity arises and when circumstances are favorable. But some of the most highly educated people are life's most renowned dunces. And some of those with scarcely any formal education at all become the most admired and ambitious contributors. Again, it's not what we have, but what we do with what we have that makes the most dramatic difference.

Never let yourself become intimidated by someone else's "education." Truly educated people will be more interested in building others than in having others' admiration. To illustrate: One year we attended a lecture where the guest speaker was an educated, successful, professional Latter-day Saint woman. Her credentials were exciting and we all believed we would glean much from her presentation. We were wrong. There was neither instruction nor inspiration. Instead, we were subjected to "when I got my master's degree this," "while I was preparing my dissertation that," and "after the completion of my doctorate then. . . ." It was a shame, but her inability to get past her "education" rendered her useless.

In comparison, another lecture was scheduled a couple of years later. The guest once again was well educated, well traveled, and articulate. Following her biographical sketch she walked up through the audience to the podium. Actually, she sort of bounced, for she was really chuckling! "I'm so sorry," she apologized for the wait, "but I got a little too preoccupied with my introduction. My, I really do sound like an interesting person! But you know," she continued seriously, "I'd forgotten about most of those things. You see, I'm the den mother in our ward, and when you work with Cub Scouts, everything else in your life seems to blend into obscurity." Immediately a bond was formed. In that brief statement the members of the audience recognized the fact that she was human, too. They saw that she recognized the same. Regardless of other things, they shared a common ground. She related; she was humble. She put her education in perspective.

We can realistically balance our dreams and aspirations with the proper values. A mother desiring to finish her education or accumulate advanced degrees may better decide to be content with Institute of Religion or extension classes, or other types of self-education, until her children are older. At that time she could more reasonably reenter the academic community. This thought seems profound in regard to our education: "If first things are first with us, then we can go on to excellence in all things."

"A time for every purpose" is fine, but what can we do *now?* Here are some possibilities that can work:

1. Believe in Relief Society. Become its advocate, participant, and contributor. A woman can say, "I got my college education in Relief Society" with a great deal of accuracy. Perhaps there is no degree, but *education* is something else again. Only an educated snob would quibble over the term *college education.*

"But I don't get anything out of Relief Society," the woman moans. Every possible form of knowledge and education is needed by women today if they are to be effective. There will never be a time in our lives when we cannot benefit in some way from a Relief Society lesson if we go with the right attitude. The teacher may or may not be able to make a lesson sing, but remember: Education, like worship, is up to the individual. If we go with an attitude of learning rather than of expecting to be entertained, we will be rewarded. After we learn we will have opportunities to share our knowledge and experience with others. In turn, we will find new areas to explore.

Perhaps you say, "Well, you can't make a silk purse out of a sow's ear. No amount of attitude can improve on the slipshod teaching and performance in my ward's Relief Society." All right, but we're talking about Relief Society, not purses. What can *you* do? Put in *your* penny's worth and crank away. In other words, do your part and do it better than it's ever been done before. Your example of excellence can rub off on others and inspire them to great things. Relief Society can serve you, fill you, enrich you, educate you, motivate and inspire you—if you serve others by participating in it!

2. Develop a talent—your private claim to fame. We all need to feel some personal accomplishment. And we should each have

an area in which we work hard to excel. It doesn't matter whether or not the activity will impress others. It matters considerably that we are able to feel an amount of personal pride. Elder Neal A. Maxwell's boyhood hobby of raising pigs makes an impressive example. I have seen a photograph of him standing with a placard of prize ribbons; the smile on his young face showed that we can, in fact, take a fabric called effort and weave it into a banner of accomplishment.

We are not sheets of carbon paper. We should develop our own talent areas, and not try to mimic others. The talents that look good on them might not look good on us! It doesn't make much sense for a woman to wear bright red lipstick if she has crooked teeth, while wearing no makeup at all on her magnificent eyes. Some of our talents are stronger or more dominant than others. We can learn to capitalize on the strong ones, and meanwhile, the weaker areas will come along. They will grow.

3. Surround yourself with energetic, positive friends. You can definitely be intimidated into feeling less terrific than you are. Depression is contagious—you can get it from others.

One Sunday after our ward's meetings a woman greeted me with, "I'm so *happy* to see you here today."

"Well, thanks, I'm happy to see you, too." I smiled.

"No, *seriously,* I dreamed last night that you died."

"Oh, no," I laughed, "do I look that bad today?"

"Really," she said with concern, "my brother dreams things, and they always come true."

"Well," I said, beginning to lose sight of the humor, "how long do I have?"

My friend conceded that she wasn't sure she had "the gift," so I went home. I was just barely ruffled, and yet my husband's comments of the previous evening rang in my ear. After watching the kids all that Saturday he had greeted me with a big hug and in a pleading (although joking) voice had said, "Promise me, *promise me,* that you'll never leave me with all these kids to raise." Hmmmm. "Am I superstitious?" I questioned in my journal. The next morning the phone rang and a friendly voice from the "Everlovely Memorial Garden" asked if I would be interested in "prearrangements." That was the last straw! I locked the doors and pulled the shades, and for several days it was Dumpsville.

None of us are so strong and positive that we're completely immune to the influence of others. Our excitement can be stifled —or completely snuffed out. If we want to be excited about our profession, doesn't it make sense to develop friendships with women who share a similar vision?

4. Have and keep role models. What greater compliment could you receive from another grown woman than her laughing, "When I grow up, I'm going to be just like you." There are multitudes of people from whom we can learn throughout our entire lifetimes. We may single out one for some particular trait, and another for a different strength, but all can serve us well. It never becomes depressing as the list of models grows—only inspiring.

5. Find your own "think tank." Take the time and learn to think. It's not as easy as it sounds. Our minds are usually so cluttered with the extraneous happenings of our lives that we rarely stop and ponder, or just let creative juices flow. Even though we may not be able to escape or isolate ourselves, we can snatch bits and pieces of time to fill the bill. My own most productive thinking time must be when I'm doing the world's most boring chore—ironing! I used to think, "Well, if I haven't ironed it by this time next year, then I'll give it to Deseret Industries—let *them* iron it." But that period of time that I once considered a complete and total waste has proved to be golden. My brain must be stimulated by the monotonous up and down, up and down. Where is your think tank?

6. Read. Seek out good books as you do good friends. If you want to learn—if you *really* want to—you need to read. Yes, there are times to do it, and it will add to you as nothing else can. Why? Because reading exercises the mind. Just as a body needs stimulation to keep in shape, or even to function well, so does the mind.

Reading helps to broaden the understanding and to sharpen recall. It helps us recognize real-life experiences that illustrate gospel principles. It's as though we take a step back and then are able to observe them firsthand. We need knowledge of scriptures and doctrine, but we don't have to study *only* scriptures. There is a wide range of reading material, secular and spiritual, that is both pleasurable and easy reading. The biographies of strong personalities help us recognize strengths and weaknesses, and the rewards and sorrows of both. The spiritual as well as social value of the classic works gives us an insight and adds richness to our everyday living.

"I hate to read," or "I'm just too slow a reader" are excuses that possibly had some validity during school days. But with the maturity gained in life, motivations become different and reading then takes on an entirely new dimension. Read something positive and worthwhile each and every day. Invest in books, borrow books, check out books from the library, but *read.*

7. "If there is anything virtuous, lovely, or of good report or praiseworthy, we seek after these things" (Thirteenth Article of Faith). Believe it. Live it. Everything worthwhile has a place in our lives. Grandma always said to us, "Learn everything you can, anytime you can, from anyone you can—there will always come a time when you will be grateful you did." (Isn't it inspiring how smart we will become with grandmotherhood?) The world is rich with all kinds of opportunity for our growth. Don't get stuck in "only home" or "only church."

Experience for yourself the joy of feeding the soul. Staring back from a frosty, stiff newspaper one dreary evening during the dead of an Alaskan winter were these words, which changed the attitude I held toward life:

> If of thy mortal goods thou art bereft,
> And from thy slender store two loaves alone to
>   thee are left,
> Sell one, and with the dole
> Buy hyacinths to feed thy soul.

> (Saadi, *Golestan*)

23

8. Dream. Dreaming gives us hope and keeps our anticipation keen. Personal, spiritual, physical, and home-related dreams should all be reevaluated from time to time, but even though it may seem forever before any of them become reality, don't give up on them. (I've redecorated our living room at least fifty times over the past ten years, and changed it around mentally as many times. Even though there still is no new furniture, it has kept the interest alive.) Dreaming offers incentive during those times it would be easy to become discouraged or bored.

Taking Care of You—Spiritually

Your spiritual dimension is what keeps all your other facets in balance. It's your lubrication. There are always going to be upheavals in life. Some will be relatively minor; others will tear your heart out. But there definitely will be times when everything seems to be falling apart physically and emotionally, and the demands from every side wear you down. It will be during those trying moments that the spiritual things can keep your life in perspective. It's the spiritual feelings that bear witness to the importance of our individual roles when no one else does. Spirituality is the strength to keep on going when we tire. Do not underestimate the power of your spiritual side; do not neglect it.

Pray more than you want to or think you need to. There is reason in the promise, "Draw near unto me and I will draw near unto you" (D&C 88:63). It offers both solace and power. Prayer, it is said, is the key to the morning and the lock of the night, but it is also the passkey to all the day's experiences. Pray many times during the day, in your heart and on your knees. Keep in touch with your Father.

At night, we ask ourselves as we report: What truth have I taught today? Have I borne my testimony to my children? Have I served someone else today and made the day a success for them? Have I fulfilled my stewardship? How have I failed, and why? How can I improve? Our Heavenly Father is deeply interested in our success.

The saying goes that if you have one true friend, you are a rich man; if you have two, you are then a king. Our true wealth is in the Savior's friendship. Experienced, it becomes a priceless thing. I knelt one year during early hours to express my gratitude for our healthy fourth baby. That particular pregnancy had been filled with worry and fear, and I just fell apart, relieved to at last unload the burden. As warmth and peace and a depth of sweetness was felt then, I caught a glimpse of the Lord's true compassion. We have an insight into that loving personality in Doctrine and Covenants 78:17-18:

> Verily, verily, I say unto you, ye are little children, and ye have not as yet understood how great blessings the Father hath in his own hands and prepared for you;
>
> And ye cannot bear all things now; nevertheless, be of good cheer, for I will lead you along. The kingdom is yours and the blessings thereof are yours, and the riches of eternity are yours.

FOUR

PRINCE CHARMING IS REALLY A MAN IN DISGUISE

Dear Mom: Well, you surely were right about one thing. Living with a man isn't anything at all like the movies. At least, most of the movies. In "Fiddler on the Roof" Tevye was close to the mark. Referring to Tzeitel and Motel he questioned, "What do they know? They're so happy they don't realize how miserable they really are."

Probably we've all heard the scientific analysis that the human body is comprised of 93 percent water, and the remaining percentage is various chemicals. The result: a man or woman. That is the ultimate in oversimplification. But if it were true, one thing would be sure. The chemicals in men would be "basic," and those in women, "complex." The probability of having them mix compatibly seems about like that of mixing water and oil. Dr. Lucille Johnson stated that men and women are so different that they not only seem to be of different species—they seem to have come from different planets. Our own experiences may support that philosophy. But truly embracing it can be difficult when we're confronted by our lifelong teachings: Marriage is ordained of God. Woman was given to man to be his helpmeet. A man should cleave unto his wife, forsaking all others. We are to become one flesh. What a pickle! Longfellow's familiar words from *Song of Hiawatha,* comparing man and woman to a bow and arrow, seem to have been inspired:

> As unto the bow the cord is,
> So unto the man is woman;
> Though she bends him, she obeys him,
> Though she draws him, yet she follows;
> Useless each without the other!

Why, then, does it seem so difficult to understand one another? Why aren't we more alike? (More specifically, why aren't men more like women?)

Men are different. That fact is first and foremost. Don't ponder it; don't fret over it. Accept it. They do not act the way women do, they do not think the way we do, and their emotions and ours are on opposite sides of the Continental Divide. Only when we're able to come to grips with this does it become easier to live with and understand them.

Men are predictable, at least. Their chemical combinations might result in many "varieties"—all within the same family— very much like different kinds of wood. One might resemble mahogany, and another pine or oak. But they are all still wood. Basically their structure will be a simple design: four-sided and sturdy. Women are nothing at all like that. We tend to have many, many sides. (We prefer to compare ourselves to diamonds.) It is the combination and character of these facets that in one way is so attractive to men and in another seems so frustrating to them.

Our wise Father in Heaven created men and women to be dependent on each other for completion. Through our combined experiences, we truly can become as one. That progress will lead us toward eternity and godhood. Marriage, with its blending of different personalities and inherent traits in parents and in children, is the sphere containing ingredients to forge us into glorified beings.

In *Don Juan,* Byron wrote, "Man's love is of man's life a thing apart, 'Tis woman's whole existence." His summation, for me, borders on inspiration. For it seems that woman's life does tend to be governed by her *emotion.* "Emotion" does not mean instability—but a gentle inheritance—given with purpose. This emotional depth inherent with motherhood is a necessary characteristic. It enables us to experience the intense love and sympathy that are a part of bearing and rearing a family. On the other hand, man seems more inclined to be ruled by a special *practicality* consistent with his priesthood responsibilities—providing, presiding, and governing. The combination of the two can result in great beauty, sensitivity, security, and order. If we did not understand and appreciate this difference, it would be impossible for us to blend our lives from a "me" into a "we" into a "one."

It's said that men go into marriage thinking their wives will never change, and women go into marriage thinking they will change their husbands. If so, we are all disillusioned! Something we should understand clearly about men: They like appreciation and praise, but will not be "redone for their own good." It may cause warfare. At the very least, they will resent it, and it probably won't work anyway. It's impossible for one person to "change" another person; true, lasting change must come from within.

Additionally, there are difficult times in store for the wife who treats her husband like another one of the children: "Your socks are in the Lost and Found Box. It will cost you one dime to get them out." We learn in our reading or lessons that if we communicate honestly—"Honey, I'm trying hard to keep things neat. Would you help me teach the kids by remembering to put your socks in the laundry?"—we will have success. It might work. It might not. Even if it doesn't, however, with this type of approach more will be gained than lost. One friend whose husband continually left a pile of socks appealed to him in such a manner. Sure enough—it didn't work. Dirty socks weren't worth battle, so she adopted the saying, "Change the things you can and learn to live with what you can't." She's still picking up socks, but he really does compensate in other ways. She always has a shiny, clean car to drive to church on Sunday.

One man may be mahogany, another one oak, and a third pine, but it seems fairly obvious that certain common patterns run through each individual grain. These patterns indicate that:

1. A man wants a *cheerful* companion. Your cheerful humor, like springs on a car, can absorb the jolts in marriage. Of course, it's no secret that men need to be "provoked to righteousness" from time to time. But that never has been properly interpreted to mean "nagged to righteousness." There probably isn't one man in ten thousand who would not voice a very intense dislike of a nagging woman—and particularly a nagging wife.

2. A man wants *support*. When our husbands spend a great deal of time away from us, or the family, we may find it amazingly easy to feel irritable and inconvenienced. We complain and act immature. It can happen to the best of us: Facing situations alone —from garbage duties to life's natural disasters—eats at us. It's hard, and we feel neglected and sorry for ourselves at times.

The mist finally cleared for me one day and I could see more clearly. Yes, Dave was gone too much. But it was a part of his personality—spiritual personality—to care for and protect us. When he wasn't home, he wasn't fishing or playing racquetball. He wasn't having a good time while I was "trapped." When gone, he was always working to support my homemaking and feed our family. He accepts that responsibility and doesn't impose it on me. It's that kind of attitude in dad that allows mother to be in the audience at the school play when other mothers find it necessary to be employed away from home.

3. A man wants *respect*. "Husbands are a sorry lot," confessed the cartoon character Dagwood. We may sigh in agreement. It can become painfully easy for a woman to find herself "disenchanted" with her Prince Charming. If he's mortal, he makes mistakes. But it's always easier to pinpoint the flaws in one's own husband, while those of others remain hidden to the eye. "The grass is always greener" attitude is an age-old problem.

In the early days of the Church there were women who requested that they be sealed to a prophet or a man they considered more worthy than their own husbands. Then, as now, many women failed to exercise faith in the priesthood of their husbands.

A certain woman was constantly hearing how lucky she was to be married to "such a fine man." Yes, he is—no doubt. He is known for his character and he holds a responsible position in the Church. People love him. But too much is too much. She finally began responding, "Yes, he is a wonderful man. And he should be—it took me twenty years to get him that way." The moral: In each husband, every one, there is a seed of godhood. We can nurture that seed. It will grow as we show him the respect his potential deserves.

4. A man wants an *efficient* wife. Life becomes much more simplified and workable if the husband functions efficiently in his role, and the wife in hers. The responsibility of running the home is generally delegated to the wife. Having to evaluate or approve her every movement places an unnecessary load on the husband. One of his most unwelcome burdens is a wife who is a poor housekeeper. From a survey taken among men, a psychologist found that the biggest complaint in marriage (following finances) was that the wife was a sloppy housekeeper. To a man's way of thinking it is simple: He should expect clean towels after a shower, be able to walk through the house in the middle of the night without fear of tripping, and find an ironed shirt in the closet in the morning. In short, he wants an efficient wife.

5. A man needs *feeding*. There are hungers much more pain inflicting than those of an empty stomach. For a man the need to have his masculine ego fed is very important. He needs to know that he is important to the woman in his life, and that all he does doesn't go unnoticed. It's vital that the spouse relationship be stable and warm, for if partners are happy with each other and with themselves, all other problems fall into proper perspective.

I once asked the advice of a neighbor with a green thumb

when my plants continually failed, and she asked what I fed them. Surprised, I replied that I watered them but had never fed them. She exclaimed, "How would *you* do if you never got fed?" Frankly, I had never thought about it. Our man-woman relationship needs a lot of feeding or it may wilt—not dying perhaps, but certainly not thriving.

We may even have to bite our tongues if we have not yet learned to "murmur not." It's inappropriate to ridicule or belittle leaders at all, but especially before our children. It's even more important that we neither ridicule nor belittle our husbands, before our children or anyone else. If we speak thoughtlessly or hastily of our husbands or of the priesthood, then we damage the credibility of the priesthood in the eyes of others. We don't appreciate it when silly, demeaning remarks are made about women. It hurts us. Careless remarks will also hurt and insult our husbands—and we both lose.

Things often don't go smoothly, of course. Sometimes we think they won't ever go smoothly. But just as the notion of falling in love at first sight is a fanciful one, so is the idea that we will never have problems. At the times when we're most tempted to share with others our frustrations about our mates, it is probably best for us not to speak at all. Time will mend many disagreements, hurts, or violations. We forget them, but most times others do not. If you do make the decision to share your burden with a friend, make sure you choose one who will not violate your confidence and who will love you even more for your faith in the friendship.

We won't always agree with our spouses, but that doesn't mean we are failures. "Ah, they were human, too," is our grateful response to President and Sister Spencer W. Kimball. Once when they could not come to a satisfactory solution as to where they should spend their vacation, he went alone—she stayed home! Disagreement happens in the most solid of relationships. But it is the exception rather than the rule in a marriage that is "fed" instead of just "watered."

"How Could He!"

"Events" are extremely important to most women. Birthdays, anniversaries, Mother's Day, all have a significant place. Many men don't see it that way. That's one difference that will probably surface sooner rather than later.

This should have been evident to me on our fifth anniversary. How *could* he, how could anyone, forget his fifth anniversary? It had meant so much to me. Dinner was his favorite. The baby was in bed. The table was set with china, crystal, and flowers, while music drifted in the background. The gift I had saved for over the previous six months was wrapped and waiting. I was wrapped and waiting! Everything was going to be *perfect!* Only one problem: Dave dragged home exhausted that night. Without even seeing the table he muttered over his shoulder, "Got to lie down; what a day!" I saw him alive the next morning, and I even spoke to him several days later.

In reality marriage may be the beginning of the end of the coy, romantic games for many men. They then may become transformed into unusually practical beings, and may seem very content with the realities and challenges dealt to them by life. Generally, most men do not like the romantic-movie-type games we find so captivating. And it could seem more like schoolgirl romanticism for us to expect they will initiate such a game themselves.

Sometimes it seems amazing that men can travel to the moon but can't remember their wives' birthdays creatively or spontaneously. Our husbands want to make us happy. It confuses them if we are disappointed. But because they are thinking in wave signals from the other side of the Milky Way, about everything in the world *except* events like anniversaries, we need to help them along the way. Most of them need to be reminded that some special day is approaching. If that day will include a celebration, we need to make the arrangements ourselves or keep dropping hints to our husbands. We need to let them know, by whatever means work best, what it is we expect.

It's your turn to be practical now. Accept your husband for the way he is and then do what's necessary to remind him: Pin notes on his pillow, tell his secretary, write it on a piece of lettuce and tuck it inside his sandwich. Incidentally: If your husband is an exception—congratulations!

Make sure specifically that your birthday and Mother's Day are remembered. Most women know the disappointment of having been either forgotten or hurt by a hasty "Happy Mother's Day, mom, now, when do we eat?" The hurt we feel, however, is not as significant as the irresponsibility we are teaching our children. This thought should be instilled in every child: "Mother is so special that on her birthday or Mother's Day she should always be remembered with thoughtfulness and some special effort." If more boys grew up in homes where this principle was lived and taught, there would be more husbands who continued the tradition in their own homes. There would be many less frustrated wives, and many more respectful and thoughtful children. It begins with mother.

Some husbands (very few, very rare, practically extinct) will remember special events by themselves. Some need only a gentle nudge, and some need hard, practical advice—step-by-step instructions, possibly. One young woman could see the writing on the wall, so to speak, after two years of marriage. She discussed frankly with her husband the fact that a birthday cake was really important to her, and she didn't relish the idea of having to make her own for the rest of her life.

She asked if he would be responsible for buying a bakery cake each year. He was really grateful for that direction. He was happy; she was happy. Again, most men want to do what will make their wives feel good, but they have trouble reading our signals. We say, "Oh, don't do anything at all," when we really want them to do something.

Apparently men endure rather than enjoy such events. Most are frustrated by them. But rather than spending years being disappointed or "sacrificing" (trying not to make it seem as important as it really is to you), assess your feelings. Then discuss them honestly with your husband. Playing the martyr will only make you think less of yourself. "If everyone forgot my birthday, I will too. After all, it's not that important"—which really means "I'm not important." But you *are* important. Your husband just needs your help along the way.

Marriages are made not only during good times, but during reality—fatigued and weary minds, overtaxed finances, colicky babies, years of heavily pregnant bodies, late hours at work or at meetings, disappointments, illnesses, mortgages and second mortgages, doing for others with little reward, weeping, teaching, repeating, hoping, praying, waiting, urging, threatening. The list is endless. Different people have said to me, "You and your husband seem so well suited. It must have been a marriage made in heaven." They're wrong—like all marriages, it's being made right here in the confusion and reality of each and every day. (And it really is worth every minute of it!)

And Baby Makes Three

Fatherhood! Now, *that* he takes *very* seriously. Fatherhood can transform a free-wheeling hot-rodder into the community's most conservative driver within a matter of months. Other transitions take a little more time. After all, why should we expect a miracle overnight? Fathers, too, need role models.

Joseph Smith was one of the noblest examples of a husband and patriarch. It is a shame we could not have known him personally. He once wrote to his wife Emma and instructed her regarding their children. Husbands will do that, you know. They spend most of their time gone, but will breeze in just long enough to give you a little "counsel" and practical advice. Sure, it's easy for him to tell you to use more patience. (Just leave him for a day and see how *he* does.) This can be a hard dose to swallow.

On those occasions, few women would feel offended if their husbands followed more closely Joseph's example. He wrote to Emma: "Do teach them all you can, that they may have good minds. Be tender and kind to them. Don't be fractious to them, but listen to their wants." And later: "Oh, my affectionate Emma, I want you to remember that I am a true and faithful friend, to you and the children, forever. My heart is intwined around you forever and ever. Oh may God bless you all." (*Ensign,* April 1977, page 12.) These short messages pack a mighty sermon.

Men respond to parenthood much differently than we women do. Their enthusiasm is often intense, but short-lived. The night we brought our first baby home was a fine example. When that first little wail came during the night, Dave leaped out of bed, saying, "There's our baby boy!" He turned on the light and the radio, fluffed some pillows, got me a glass of juice, and brought the baby. What attentiveness! That was the end. When the little wail repeated itself the second night, Dave turned over in his sleep, put the pillow over his head, and didn't hear another cry in the night from any of the next five children. Always he has been uncomplaining and willing to help in the night—once awakened. Otherwise, two thousand Union troops marching through the streets of Atlanta could not bring him to life. It is a mystery.

Still, the "daddy" side can be the most delightful one of a man's personality. Particularly, a father who brings his priest-hood blessing home is like no other father in the world. How loved he truly is!

Note: There seems to be a common feeling shared by many women that can be summed up in one sentence: "So tell it to my husband!" If you feel this way, turn to the next chapter and hand the book over to him.

FIVE

FOR YOU, KIND SIR

This book, kind sir, is for women. So why was it thrust into your unwaiting hands? Because, wonderful though you may be, you need it. You may think you have your wife figured out, but you are probably wrong. At the very least, it's no secret to you that women are not the easiest creatures to understand. Some men are devastated to think they may never have their wives analyzed; others accept it in stride. True, we women are frustrating. We admit it. We are many times unstable, perplexing, as well as annoying. But women have the ability like nothing else to bring a softness and beauty into your pragmatic world.

Now, what do you *really* understand about a woman's make-up? About this much:

Of course, there's always hope. There are times that your practical eyes can zoom in like a television camera and capture a very accurate image. However, that image is a small part of a super-cinema-sized screen, while the average man's "camera capacity" is about fifteen inches. There's a lot more to the entire picture than you're able to get at any one time!

The saying "It takes one to know one" is true. And since a woman is probably best understood by another woman, may I remind you (from the feminine perspective) about what may seem to be some twists in your wife's personality? These are things that seem so basic to us as women that it's difficult for us to grasp why men don't hold them in the same high esteem.

1. A woman needs *love*. This is *basic.* Her idea of love, though, is very different from yours. We are not made the same, and we don't think the same. She emotionally would like your total, complete, undivided loyalty and attention. Now, you probably think that seems unreasonable. Looking at it rationally, so would she—she is not always rational. That is the reason your wife can sometimes become sad or complaining. She may say your profession or church assignments seem to come first in your life, before her.

Man and woman do not see things from a mutual vantage point. That's true on practically every issue! Admitting that helps you understand and appreciate her rationale. You will find that she becomes much more understanding and supportive if you take the time to share your dreams, visions, and goals with her. "Why should I have to explain the obvious?" you question. Because, no matter how obvious it may seem to you, you need to share it with her *verbally* from time to time.

A woman feels most loved when she is treated gently and sweetly and tenderly. Again, we approach things from different directions. For a woman, the most intense sensation of being loved comes through her emotional levels rather than through physical ones. It's more natural for a man to show the intensity of his feelings physically, so it's not easy for him to appreciate this difference. You love her, so you come and wrap around her. She bristles. "What's the problem?" you question. She doesn't feel "loved," is her response. Puzzling, isn't she?

Women particularly need to *hear* the word "love" more than most men use it. From your standpoint it seems obvious: Everything you do, all you work for is to show her how important she is. But, from her vantage point—it needs to be *heard!*

Your wife will react to your thoughtfulness. Big gestures are fine—but it's those little things that seem to count most. She may respond with what seems out-of-proportion gratitude because of something you did—and you won't even know what it was! Now, why do "little things" cause such an outpouring of attention? Because to a woman such attentiveness says, "You are loved."

Remember, your wife's qualities of sensitivity do not become less with the passing of time. If anything, they increase through her motherhood. Sensitivities should blossom in womanhood. Unfortunately, there are too many times they do not blossom. Even so, they are still within—quiet and deep. If those sensitivities are abused or threatened, most women will not let them die quietly. The reaction may be abrasive or aggressive. It's not intentional; it is merely the natural defense mechanism within her that defends her womanhood.

2. A woman needs to maintain *femininity.* There's no doubt that both men and women are physically capable of doing certain tasks, such as taking out garbage, cleaning garages, changing the oil, and so on. But you will come out way ahead if you accept this type of chore as your responsibility. Helping you cut and haul firewood can be exhilarating for her, but if that type of activity becomes solely her responsibility, her femininity may seem lessened. It may dull her. That is because those types of activities minimize rather than enhance her eternal nature.

Little boys reach a certain age when they become frustrated and angry because they want "man jobs" to do. It's the same with women. Many times a woman's not acting feminine may be traceable to the fact that she is not truly treated in a feminine way. If you delegate to her such tasks as fixing the disposal, replacing the screens or washers, or even taking the mower to the repairman, you may be surprised at her reaction: It may be one of anger, criticism, or independence. Even though it's difficult for a woman to admit even to herself, she may quietly feel that a man would not place this particular type of burden upon his wife if he truly honored womanhood. This is not always true, of course, but you may want to step back and analyze whether it might apply in your home. A man who respects his wife's eternal role will not expect and in many cases should not allow her to perform tasks that are not conducive to femininity.

3. A woman needs personal *space* for individuality, growth, and development. Your wife needs your support for her homemaking, of course. But she especially needs to be appreciated as more than the creator of small bodies or the keeper of the castle. She needs to grow! A wife doesn't hear the click of a time clock. Her hours are all hours. And without some preventive maintenance along the way, she may become a victim of "burnout." That maintenance is not optional or merely for those who are "weak." *Every* woman must have it. Without it, she will droop and become ineffective. One wife was trying to express this need to her husband but was not met by an understanding heart or listening ear. Instead, she was assaulted with: "Well, what do you do all day long anyway? When you start earning as much as I do, or do the kind of work I have to, then come and talk to me." Is there any wonder that that relationship was one-sided and rocky? What a vast difference between "preside" and "rule"!

Where does the responsibility lie? With *you*. A man is patriarch of his home. The sanctification of his family unit is his priesthood responsibility. Just as the wife oversees the attitudes and development of children, he should oversee and monitor her attitude and growth. He should take the responsibility, if necessary, to make sure she recharges. Husbands and families have an equal responsibility to support the wife and mother in her personal quests, as she supports them in theirs.

Carol Lynn Pearson wrote a poem called "The Steward" that poignantly detailed one husband's error in this area. Taking his last look at the fields of the family farm, Heber considers with satisfaction the stewardship he has exercised over them. His wife, Margaret, is inside doing the packing for their move to a condominium. She comes upon her old violin, and tears come to her eyes as she remembers the chance she had to play with a symphony orchestra in town and her appeal to her husband to let her. But he didn't see it as she did. As "steward" over her life, he considered it his responsibility to keep her at home—where she belonged. Ignoring the sacrifices she offered to make in order to realize her dream, he forbade her to join the orchestra. And gradually she withered. "He didn't really notice how it happened —/the shrinking of her borders,/the drying up of her green."

Outside, Heber is contemplating facing his long-dead father with his stewardship report:

> Heber gave a last look at his lands
> And he was pleased.
> He could face his father with a clear mind.
> "Here's my stewardship," he would say,
> "And I think you'll find
> I did everything you asked.
> I took what you gave me—and I made it more."
>
> (From *The Growing Season,* Bookcraft, 1976)

Author Rodney Turner summed it up by saying that a "priesthood husband" will respect his wife's right to her own identity and will be pleased when she expresses her desires and interests in ways that will enable her to grow, to take what she has and make it more. A priesthood husband, the author continues, knows that his wife "has needs which leap the walls of home and go bounding off across the fields." He recognizes these needs of the inner woman as facets of her personality that are an inheritance from her heavenly parents. Man can and should be "the vehicle through which sanctification comes to his companion." (*Woman and the Priesthood* [Salt Lake City: Deseret Book Co., 1972], page 302.)

4. A woman needs *support* for her profession. Dickens's masterpiece *A Tale of Two Cities* begins with a simple sentence:

"It was the best of times—it was the worst of times." This capsule statement is true today for women. It truly is the best of times—for development opportunities and education. But it is also the worst of times. There has never been a period of time when more pressure has been placed upon a woman to reevaluate her values and goals. Her profession of wife and mother is one that she inherited with marriage. It may have caused her to leave educational and career pursuits before she had planned. Though it was the right thing to do, it can still cause turmoil in some women, and particularly when they are made to seem unimportant by their husbands.

It can be difficult for a woman to accept her husband's right to an option in occupational choice when she sees no such option for herself. The rightness or wrongness of this attitude isn't what's important here: The fact is that it's true for many. To add fuel to her potential fire is the fact that she is confronted at every turn to reconsider those priorities. Professionals, neighbors, the media, economic factors, even relatives (and saddest, even some husbands)—all urge her to place things of the world before things of eternal value. This may cause some mental turmoil for even the stalwart. In any case, the wife needs an ally. She needs your support for her profession. She needs to know that you feel that her role is a vital and important one.

A "priesthood husband" (one who presides and doesn't rule, who leads by example and doesn't drag) should be more admired than any man alive. He supports his family not only financially, but emotionally and spiritually as well. He should be saluted and honored. With the never-ending rise in costs of food, clothing, housing, medical care, education, missions, and everything, the task seems horrendous. Some men are grateful to relinquish some of that responsibility to their working wives. What a blessing it is to know that a "priesthood husband" will shoulder that extreme-ly difficult task.

Some women choose for themselves to enter the work force. Reasons vary, and it wouldn't be possible to make a blanket statement to cover every situation. Suffice it to say that the choice to stay in the home is not met positively in many areas of our world. The husband's emotional support is a critical factor in this choice.

5. A woman needs her husband's *respect*. How frustrating and confusing it is for a woman to hear over and over again what an elevated position she holds in the eternal scheme of things when she is treated like a second-class citizen by those in her own home. A child by and large treats his mother the same way the father does. But even when he has a positive example, he may still develop gargantuan nerve when dad is gone. Plainly stated, a father should never tolerate disrespect toward his wife from the children. And he should intercede immediately if they are verbally abusing her. The father is the one to let all family members know that, regardless of their age, punishment for such an offense will be swift.

Sadder still is to witness such abuse from the husband. A man's subjecting his wife to "wife jokes" is in the poorest taste. Such jokes have no place in the humor of a priesthood husband. Even "in fun" they are demeaning—to both the woman and the offender. They cut her deeply and that hurt lingers. It seems hypocritical to hear a man say in one breath that he loves and honors his wife and in the next breath offer a typical, "I'd buy my wife a new dust cloth, but then I'd have to hire someone to show her how to use it."

Our Father in Heaven holds his daughters in particularly lofty regard. Those who abuse the ones whom even the Eternal Father has chosen to protect with his priesthood will surely be called to account. The women of the Church should speak respectfully of the priesthood at all times, and they have every right to expect such courtesy from the men in the Church. Latter-day Saint women should always hold priesthood in respect; priesthood should always defend womanhood.

6. A woman needs *appreciation*. Consider the message found in the book of Proverbs:

> Who can find a virtuous woman? for her price is far above rubies.

42

The heart of her husband doth safely trust in her, so that he shall have no need of spoil.

She will do him good and not evil all the days of her life.

She seeketh wool, and flax, and worketh willingly with her hands.

She is like the merchants' ships; she bringeth her food from afar.

She riseth also while it is yet night, and giveth meat to her household, and a portion to her maidens.

She considereth a field, and buyeth it: with the fruit of her hands she planteth a vineyard.

She girdeth her loins with strength, and strengtheneth her arms.

She perceiveth that her merchandise is good: her candle goeth not out by night.

She layeth her hands to the spindle, and her hands hold the distaff.

She stretcheth out her hand to the poor; yea, she reacheth forth her hands to the needy.

She is not afraid of the snow for her household: For all her household are clothed with scarlet.

She maketh herself coverings of tapestry; her clothing is silk and purple.

Her husband is known in the gates, when he sitteth among the elders of the land.

She maketh fine linen, and selleth it; and delivereth girdles unto the merchant.

Strength and honour are her clothing; and she shall rejoice in time to come.

She openeth her mouth with wisdom; and in her tongue is the law of kindness.

She looketh well to the ways of her household, and eateth not the bread of idleness.

Her children arise up, and call her blessed; her husband also, and he praiseth her.

Many daughters have done virtuously, but thou excellest them all.

Favour is deceitful, and beauty is vain: but a woman that feareth the Lord, she shall be praised.

Give her of the fruit of her hands; and let her own works praise her in the gates. (Proverbs 31:10-31.)

Why was this superwoman able to accomplish such feats? What was the key? Look at verse 28: "Her children arise up, and call her blessed; her husband also, *and he praiseth her.*" Praise is reward, and reward is a great incentive to activity. If you were to come home one evening and announce that in twenty-four hours you would be leaving for ten days in the Caribbean and wanted your wife to go—you would be amazed to see just what a superwoman your own wife really is.

Rewards do work miracles. And appreciation works the same way. We mothers will take the crumbs of appreciation that come from children, but we need something much more substantial from our husbands. For instance, if she is dieting, your wife doesn't need you to snatch a potato chip out of her mouth. She needs you to express some appreciation that she is trying. It would be 100 percent more effective to instead tell her, with a little hug, how cute she's looking. With some encouragement and praise, she will throw the bag of chips away herself without a word. The same holds true in all areas of her life. A woman who is treated like the queen of the home will act the part.

A woman wants her husband to support her personal quests as well as her professional one. She wants him to remind her of her weaknesses and yet point out her strengths. She will respond to a man who is patient and willing to accept her as she is while helping her to become the best she can. She responds with love, commitment, and indisputable loyalty to a man who values her. From the feminine vantage point a husband is never more manly than when kneeling in prayer, never more mature than when he's able to hold a burping baby to his lapel, and never more appreciated than when he insists that his wife escape and "recharge" while he assumes home responsibilities with a smile—and then tells her he couldn't do it without her! He sets an example of excellence for his wife and for his family by his work and attitude. Your willingness to support your wife in these ways will enhance her view of your masculinity, and your role in her life. She truly will embrace the Lord's counsel to Emma Smith: "Let thy soul delight in thy husband—" (D&C 25:14).

You are the key ingredient to your wife's success or failure. When things are right between you, all else falls into place. It seems that life can become so involved for you professionally, and for her with home and children (and the Church for you both), that the tender cord binding you together can easily become obscured. And yet, throughout life's confusion, her bond to you remains as it was. That is woman's nature. Her commitment is total.

This "wish" transformed an applicant into the winner of a luxury cruise: "I would like to win this cruise because after fifteen years of being a mother to Jill, Terry, Michael, and Shawn, and the keeper of Patches, Muffins, Murphy, and Bun-Bun, for a glorious little while I could just be Doug's sweetheart again."

SIX

ROBBING PETER TO PAY PAUL

Dear Mom: Just tell me this: If I'm smart enough to handle the silver coin, then why am I sitting here eating the kids' peanut-butter-and-jelly crusts while he's eating out on the expense account? (Not really!) Sometimes I just don't seem rational when it comes to money. The scriptures are right, it is filthy lucre!

"It's only money!" That statement minimizes money's place in our lives to a fault. Even in the best of relationships, money problems can cause strain. Many times we bring the grief upon ourselves, but that grief can be lessened considerably if we remember this: The money earned from a man's profession is *mutual pay.* It belongs to both husband and wife. They both should have the responsibilities and privileges that are connected with it.

Providing money is only part of a man's responsibility to provide for his family, just as maintaining the home is only part of a woman's job description. Both should keep their eyes wide open and their wits about them when staring at the coin purse. A man should not feel that after earning the income he is then able to walk away from additional responsibilities. Because it's a relatively simple thing to "hand over the paycheck" without helping to determine how it will be used, a man simply may not be aware of the additional strain this may create for his wife. And from her point of view, the strain may seem futile. For if the provider feels the pinch and the juggle, psychologically if nothing else, at least he knows he has earning power. This knowledge puts light at the end of the tunnel. But that's impossible for the wife. When the financial demands are severe she may feel emotionally trapped because she is incapable of finding a solution to fill the needs. Money management should be a shared responsibility.

A wife should have a budget to work within, and she should be financially responsible with that amount. I love President Barbara Smith's consistent use of the word *provident*. To be considered a provident person is a compliment. It indicates someone with wisdom. But being known as "cheap" indicates just that. Being "cheap" easily may lead to selfishness. Provident living helps us become wise. Our capacity to be even more generous then grows. Cheap is a state of our pocketbooks, but provident is a state of our outlook (involving some ability, of course).

We all have to live with financial limitations, and both husband and wife need to be realistic about these. A bargain is no bargain if there's no money in the bank. The "I saved you $150 today by spending only $75 at a great sale" idea doesn't hold much water if there's only $25 left until payday. On the other hand, a man has to be reasonable about what he expects his wife to accomplish. A woman told how her husband gave her less than thirty dollars to buy groceries for two weeks, plus pay the "household" expenses. But he still had money left for sports and pets. That's not only unfair, it is absolutely ridiculous.

A woman should be expected to learn the art of provident living, but her husband shouldn't expect that she can squeeze blood from a turnip. A dollar will buy only a dollar's worth of commodities. Even the most frugal wife can do only so much! And the other side of the coin applies as well: A man should be expected to do his utmost to provide adequately for his family's needs, but his wife shouldn't act as though he's printing currency in the basement.

Part of the provider's responsibility is that he be as considerate of his family's needs and his wife's personal needs as possible. He should be as generous as their circumstances permit. While being provident, a wife should not feel that she can never buy anything for herself. This is both unfair and frequently demeaning—and it is not even good for those for whom she is "sacrificing."

Carol Lynn Pearson depicts this situation in her poem "Millie's Mother's Red Dress." The poem has a woman on her deathbed telling her daughter how futile it had been for her to always put others' needs before her own. The one time she had done something for herself—bought a beautiful dress—her family had ridiculed her and shamed her out of wearing it ever again.

This woman's "unselfishness" had bred dependency and selfishness in her family, as they had learned to continually take and never give. "Oh, Millie," she mourns,

> I always thought if you take
> Nothing for yourself in this world,
> You'd have it all in the next somehow.
> I don't believe that anymore.
> I think the Lord wants us to have something—
> Here—and now.
>
> (From *The Growing Season*, Bookcraft, 1976)

Is this example extreme? Probably so. Is its underlying feeling the exception? Probably not.

I would be rich if I had a nickel for every comment I've heard like: "I spent ten dollars on (whatever) . . . oh, how will I ever tell my husband?" "He would just kill me if . . . ." "I'm so tired of not having anything in our home. We need so many things, but he seems determined to save us into the poorhouse." Realistically, financial disagreements are not necessarily his fault—or yours.

They are a rut we get into. And there are eleven letters on the ladder to climb out of it: c-o-m-m-u-n-i-c-a-t-e.

The essential first step: You've got to open your mouth. This sounds easy, but for many it is not. Many women never open their mouths regarding things that really matter to them for fear it might bring contention. What it will bring is communication. And even communication with some contention is still better than no communication at all, for then we are at least applying the principles that can be made to work correctly. We can each be completely forthright and honest and at the same time follow the Psalmist's example, "We took sweet counsel together" (Psalm 55:14). That is the point of bedrock. It is the beginning of success.

If the surface is merely scratched, and bedrock is never reached, it might indicate a more serious problem than just a financial one. At the point when the partner controlling the purse strings uses that power to intimidate or control the other, flashing lights should go off: Insecure, insecure, insecure! Both need outside help—run, don't walk, for it.

Before leaving this subject, there is another incidental worth mentioning. It is the misnomer we call "grocery money." If all we bought with grocery money was groceries, we would all be eating like kings. In most households there are other strings attached to that fund. "Grocery money" is often expected to cover such items as school expenses, music or dancing lessons, clothing, household maintenance, gas for the car, tuition for classes, sports uniforms, birthday presents, fertilizer, and so on.

A wife, out of necessity, is probably more realistic about what the grocery money is supposed to purchase because she's the one who deals with the daily "nit-pick." She should make sure her husband gets the entire picture, or it isn't fair to either one of them. A man may smile broadly and brag, "You should see what my wife can do with a dollar," while she is really pulling her hair out in frustration.

Finally, earning power does not give carte blanche spending

power. Many times a household income is completely blown apart by the husband's buying expensive tools, guns, vacation equipment, and other spur-of-the-moment purchases. It is not the norm for a woman to include in her spontaneous purchases the equivalent types of items: new furniture, appliances, or jewels. When it comes to major expenses, the decisions should always be joint ones.

SEVEN

SAY "MAMA"

*Oh, Mom! The books were right! Insanity is hereditary. It's
the direction they were wrong about. You get it from your kids!*

If there is any area of life that we all face unrealistically, it is
parenting. (After all, it's a well-accepted fact that no one is really
prepared to parent until it's twenty-five years too late!) But a
simple formula for looking more realistically at family life might
be: The reality of living with children is that the normal is really
the abnormal, and vice versa.

We are deluded if we think that family life will always
mean clean houses, immaculate, smiling mothers, and freshly
scrubbed, cheerful children. For most of us, that vision has long
since gone up in smoke. (It generally doesn't take long!) We are
learning to live in the "real" world, where mother walks across a
floor covered with Krunchy Korn Krisps after the morning bed-
lam of sending a family of children off to school. The real world
for a family generally means a child who dresses the cat instead of
himself before school, one who tattoos his stomach with a
ballpoint pen instead of finding his shoes, and another who
habitually has either a jelly bean or piece of popcorn stuck in his
ear. In the real world mommies and daddies borrow money from

their children and not the other way around, dad seems relieved to be off to work, and children pretend they do not know her as mother throws kisses after them.

A wise mother doesn't (often) overreact. After a typically hectic morning, she may sit down and merely smile.

It's significant that mother doesn't scream or become frustrated. She doesn't run to the psychologist or to the bishop. She sits calmly and smiles. A wise mother undoubtedly has learned the lesson that because these unpredictable things happen (or are they really predictable?) it doesn't mean the end of the world. It does not make her look a failure as a mother. It's life.

You know how kids are. They never walk as fast or as slowly as you want them to. They never need to go to the bathroom until you have unpacked at the park. They'll rehearse their little talk every day for two weeks and then completely clam up at the podium. But in the shopping mall they can screech at the top of their lungs, "Look at the fat lady!" Little Bubba won't ever be able to find two socks that match—until Easter, when he marches into the chapel wearing fire-engine-red soccer socks! And, of course, we all know that children's memories are an inch long when it comes to remembering where they left their new coats. But they have memories like elephants when *"You promised!"* In the beginning we coax them, " 'Mama,' come on honey, say 'Mama.' " But it doesn't take too long until we wished no one knew the meaning of the word. Have you ever wondered why we are given the counsel to have "patience *and* long-suffering"? Because patience probably won't work, and we will have to rely on long-suffering to make it through the epic event of raising children.

Truly, it isn't easy being the mother of a large family. There are always people, for example, who make "comments" as our little train of ducklings follow behind. Of course, these are always moments when a duckling doesn't perform as expected. One day a very pregnant friend of mine took her four little ones to an ice-cream parlor. There she encountered one of "those people"— the ones who keep dropping hints about "inconsiderate people overpopulating the world," or "Honestly, you would think some people have enough already!" Now, this is where the books tell how you will be able to smile as all your well-mannered children contentedly lick their cones. Unfortunately, the youngest girl hadn't read any of those books! Instead, she stomped up to the offensive woman, looked her straight in the eye, and plunged a spoon into her hot-fudge sundae. That woman didn't laugh (and neither did my little friend's mother!)—but oh, I did!

Generally, as our children are well pressed and well behaved, we can walk with our heads held high. The comments will still come, of course, and never more than when the mother of "all those kids" is expecting another one. But we know what's really important.

Only days away from baby number four I caught a case of cabin fever. It was so severe that we braved a subzero blizzard to get to the local discount store. After all, there were drastic shortages that couldn't wait (kiddie barrettes, Mod Podge, and molly screws). Into the snowsuits, mittens, boots, and hats my three toddlers and I tumbled (in my shape about that time, I mean tumbled!), and off we went. After the "breather" among real people over three feet tall, I made my selections and proceeded to stand in the check-out line.

As every mother knows, there's a point of no return in every check-out lane. You can neither retreat (because of those behind you), nor advance (in hopes of a quick, emergency exit). In other words—you're trapped. This, of course, is when the children fall out of formation. All of a sudden one is pulling the fuzzy ball on top of another's hat so that the ties are making her face turn blue (not too blue to stifle a scream). Then another grabs a handful of gum and mints and stuffs them into her mouth. The oldest one falls over the side of the basket and hangs upside down by his knees. Any semblance of order disappeared about three howls and one box of spilled screws ago. At times like this people choose to either ignore you or stare contemptuously. I cried in the car that day and swore I would never take my children *anywhere* for at least fifteen years.

But I did. We were all tripping through the Seattle airport at dawn only a short six months later. It had been an "exciting" five-hour plane ride with four wide-awake preschoolers. It was then that my sanity and gratitude returned as a kindly traveler approached my husband and said, "What a sweet little family you have!" (Why, tell me *why,* do they always tell your husband?)

Even though they seem much longer, there are only a few years of continually taking one or all back and forth from sacrament meetings for "time out." It's trying, to be sure. And, of course, these are usually the years when your husband is in the bishopric. He sits on the stand most of the time—and smiles. Is it worth the three hours of preparation just to spend three hours in the foyer? "If they just learn that this is where they are supposed to be . . ." I would tell myself.

Those years passed quickly, it seems in retrospect. Now I smile to myself with empathy and understanding for my sisters as I watch them march out—knuckles white with pulling children six inches off the ground. When someone says, "Your children behave—you even listen to the speakers. How'd you do it?" I just want to burst out laughing, start crying, throw my arms around the person's neck, and kiss both cheeks for such a comment. We persist, fall, and get up and try again. The time passes, and sure enough, things fall into place. Then, fortunately, as in childbirth, the pains go away and we relish the reward.

"Having a family should be like cooking pancakes," grandma used to say. "Make the first one, throw it away, and then start on the good batch." We not only can't but wouldn't want to throw away our first efforts—they are so special. But we surely do make a lot of mistakes along the way, no matter how enthusiastic or diligent we try to be. Fortunately, despite what we end up doing to them, our little ones are fairly resilient and seem to come through it. They are made of good stuff.

A woman can get so much more from life's experiences if she can admit that she's not the "Model Mormon Mother." Real progress starts at that point. There's only one "Model Mormon

Mother"—she's alive and well in Fantasyland. Yes, she exists in the mind and absolutely nowhere else. There is one exemplar, however—the Savior. Children were precious to him, and despite the magnitude and gravity of his mission, he said, "Suffer the little children to come unto me" (Mark 10:14). As he dealt with people (*his* children), the Lord showed traits that we as mothers need to make our own: slowness to anger, patience, understanding. He loved, built, disciplined, taught, forgave, and led. We truly can learn from his example the significance of our role as teachers and motivators.

Overcoming differences in marriage is an essential step toward exaltation, and so is our growth in parenthood. Two people can make a baby, it is said, but only a baby can make them into parents. The family is the training ground—for children, and for parents as well.

The demand of mothering is constant and the work both perplexing and difficult. Many mothers leave the role of child rearing for those reasons. Perhaps no one told them how taxing it would truly be. They may then leave their children and assign the business of teaching them to others—family, neighbors, play schools, friends, and even television. Let's not give the training of our children to someone else, even though it is difficult work. We will learn some of our greatest lessons in training our children; we will receive and be edified together.

EIGHT

A KID IS A KID IS A KID

. . . and Mom, I never really appreciated it when you screamed, "When you grow up, I hope you have one just like you!" Do I ever appreciate it now!

"It certainly looks as though you are pregnant," the doctor announced with a broad smile. At that moment it was impossible to realize what an impact those words would have on our lives. Even if someone had tried to shed some light, we wouldn't have believed it, anyway. It would have seemed absurd. Why, just hearing that magic sentence seemed to make the weeks of throwing up worth it. And I suppose it's just as well. Once the curtain goes up, the role must be played out, and every amount of idealism and enthusiasm will be well employed in mothering.

What couple hasn't enthusiastically tried to capture the vision of what lies ahead? And when the chubby little creation arrives, what new mother is able to gaze into those baby blues and see coming in the next few years a smart-mouthed kid? (If we give it a thought at all, we think, "Oh, it won't happen to *me*.") That's the trouble with having babies—they are babies for such a short time, and they are children for *so long*. Who hasn't anxiously anticipated those freckle-faced little boys with their scuffed sneakers and toothless grins? Who hasn't itched to have an adorable little girl with tiny ponytails and ruffled panties? What we don't see in the meantime is the "continuing saga."

What has happened? It took such a short amount of time to get from the thrill of our firstborn all the way to our wit's end. What happens is simply that our babies are growing up, and we all have to experience the growing pains along the way. That baby I took such pleasure in bathing and powdering turned somehow into such a slouch. He almost has me believing that socks feel better after they've been worn for six days in a row.

Of course, children will give us fleeting visions of hope. They may occasionally volunteer to bathe, for example. Oh, they will maintain to the end that they really aren't dirty—but the bottom of the bathtub will resemble a swamp. Then arrives the day that they flip to the alter ego: Suddenly they are Mr. Cleans! It's then (knowing full well we would never do anything to discourage this twist of fate) that they plead for a shampoo guaranteed to make their hair smell terrific—the kind that costs three dollars an ounce. Then they shampoo the dog with it. They'll insist on clean jeans twice a day, but a plea to launder their favorite jersey will be met by an indignant look and a muttered, "Can you believe *her!*" There will be tears and tantrums, foot-stomping and theatrics to rival those of Sarah Bernhardt. There's an endless stream of their famous last words: "You like her better than me!" "You never did understand me!" "When I leave home," and (the one I like), "You adults have such dirty minds!"

Yes, the reality of living with children is far from the dreams we cherish while nestling that first tiny one. And the fact that we are Latter-day Saints will not change that. The fact that they are the "Youth of Zion" will not change that. But all in all, despite all their stubbornness, finagling, unpredictable ways, and just plain *crust*—kids really are nice people.

Ideally, children should be our crowning achievement, but sometimes they seem more like a pain in the neck. They, without a doubt, are individuals. There isn't one parent in the world that can predict with absolute assurance, "My child will never . . . ," for they are free agents. Their progression will be according to their own degree of commitment. Yet, because we recognize their worth and potential, we want to do everything we can for them. We lead and teach and hope and pray they will choose to continue in righteous paths. Realistically, then, what can we do to increase the probability of their success (and our sanity)?

1. Accept them.

> Here's to the kids who are different—
> The kids who don't always get A's
> The kids who have ears
> Twice the size of their peers,
> Or have noses that go on for days.
> Here's to the kids who are different—
> The kids who are just out of step,
> The kids they all tease
> Who have scrapes on their knees
> And whose sneakers are constantly wet.
> Here's to the kids who are different—
> The kids with a mischievous streak
> For when they are grown,
> As history has shown,
> It's their difference that makes them unique.
>
> (Authorship unknown)

When I first heard this little poem years ago, I could not possibly appreciate its real beauty: At that time I had no children of my own. Now, I don't laugh at it, I laugh with it.

Wouldn't it be nice if kids were at least alike? Whether good or bad, we at least would know what was coming and which battle plan to best apply. Not only is each child different, but each sex adds a new dimension. When talking about his seven children, a man said he at least knew from the beginning what each of his six boys would be like. With that little girl, he never knew from day to day what to expect. Each child presents an entirely new personality, and while we may laughingly keep blaming it on "your side of the family"—what you see is what you get.

I'm frankly taken aback when a child sits down to his favorite dinner of spaghetti and meatballs and looks upon it with utter disdain, then announces to the family that he is henceforth a vegetarian. Fine! Great! But will he leave well enough alone! No, he has to make it miserable for everyone else. (We all obviously lack his degree of intestinal fortitude.) He points out emotionally to his brother, "That meatball used to be someone's little pet." To his sister he snootily prophesies, "Starchy spaghetti will gum up your insides." Patience, mother!

It takes time. I guess that's why the Lord usually sends us only one child at a time. It takes time to realize that one child, for instance, doesn't have to be good at everything. It takes time to accept that another isn't going to share your enthusiasm for the viola—he wants to play the spoons! The interests and talents of one may be totally different than those of the family back four generations. But we need to be grateful for each one. Not every child will be musical, not every one will be a scholar or an athlete. But it's their individuality that adds strength to the family. It would be sad for the different one to regard himself as the weak link. There are children who are conformists: They do everything in exactly the right way and at the correct time. But the one riding the "wild horse" is just as loved and appreciated—sometimes even more.

We are maturing when we learn not to label as "successes" only children that act and speak according to our expectations. It's an insecure parent who is driven to have his child involved in everything to show the rest of the world how wonderful he is. Each child in every family has some strong area; we can try to appreciate that and give the child encouragement to march confidently to the beat within. He can use that positive side of his personality to support righteous principles and to build the Lord's kingdom. We can quit making comparisons! Every talent can be worthwhile and useful.

Our challenge is not to produce a society of "acceptable" clones; it is to provide homes where each personality can grow and develop in the way meant for him by Heavenly Father. It won't be a home for only the musician, but for the athlete, the scholar, the compassionate and tenderhearted, and yes, for the wayward, too. In what other home would you place him where more love and effort could be spent?

It is definitely easy to zero in on children's problem areas—probably because those are the areas that zero in on us. It truly is hard for mother to stop and remember how Jeremy says his prayers faithfully, when she is staring at the contents of his pockets after the wash: a mountain of roly-poly corpses. And it's hard to focus on the spirit of generosity when Nancy volunteers to bring all the treats for seventy-five children—again!

When faced with children's most irritating characteristics, it is a trick to keep utmost in our minds their real worth. It takes particular effort. We have to make ourselves focus on that consistent and valiant spiritual nature during the times she sits whining with a blanket over the top of her head. That outburst of "I just can't *stand*_____! (fill in the blank: (a) you, (b) brother or sister, (c) family, (d) teacher, (e) all of the above) really doesn't compare to the goodness that winds its way through the warp and woof.

Outbursts are just occasional flaws in the fabric of our children's personalities. (Sometimes a piece of fabric can look hopeless, but the right touch can turn it into a thing of beauty.) True, we have to help them overcome themselves. But remember throughout that the real beauty of design comes from the worthy characteristics. Look for the good, and accept them for both what they are and what they can be. They are children of God—the thought can't be overused or overemphasized.

2. Praise them. "Do you like me better after I go to bed than before, mommy?" That question can be thought-provoking. And sometimes we may not even have to think about it before answering, "Yes, I do!" It really is a lot easier to feel the swelling love as we gaze down on those sweetly sleeping wonders than it was during the hour before bed. Little Tommy is more lovable asleep than when he was threatening the life of his sister just because she cleaned her turtle bowl with his toothbrush. And while we keep hoping that a lovely butterfly will emerge from the cocoon around each one, what we find many times is that the

little acorn is growing into a nut! Notwithstanding these things, each and every child has a deep need for praise, and not just any praise—*our* praise. It feeds them, and they grow.

As teachers we all use praise techniques in the classroom. But it's at home, more than anywhere else, where we should clothe our kind thoughts in warm words. Even a little message written on a hard-boiled egg in the lunch sack can push a child upward. (There's a lot to be said for a warm note in a cold lunch.) Praise, though, should be honest.

As adults we don't go about publishing our own weaknesses. We would rather be known for our strengths. Why, then, would we shout from the rooftops our children's weaknesses? Instead, we should speak well of our children, becoming their advocates instead of just more critics. (There are already enough of those.) Certainly we shouldn't be blind to their faults. They all have them. But there are times when a word of support from mom can calm a rocking boat. By supporting instead of demeaning she will be more equipped to help a child strengthen the weak points and become better.

Praising our children must be differentiated from bragging about them, however. The latter can easily be carried too far. For example: We have six absolutely beautiful children. They are talented beyond our wildest dreams, and intelligent far beyond their years. They are personable, witty, and display abundant leadership qualities. Their father and grandparents would say that this is a realistic and fair appraisal. But then, how many parents don't feel pretty much the same about their children? It's wonderful that most of us do. But there is a big difference between speaking well of our children and bragging to the rest of society about them.

The more we brag, the less impressed others become with our children—and with us as well. The philosopher Goethe said: "That man is so dull. If he were a book, I would not read him." We each have wonderful talents to share, but if we don't have some humility (especially about our darling, gifted, talented ones), we can easily become "unreadable" to those around us.

The truth is that others simply are not interested in being constantly subjected to our children's glowing merits. Believe it or not, their kids are just as special! When grandma recollected how beautiful and intelligent my own mother had been as a child, she mused, "But then, I wonder how ugly she would have had to be before I wouldn't have thought she was beautiful?"

One woman recalled that as a child she asked her mother why she never bragged about them the way So-and-So did about her family. The mother wisely replied, "I don't have to brag about any of you. The way you are speaks loudly enough." People are fully capable of making their own observations and drawing their own conclusions.

Of course, the saddest example is found at the opposite end of the spectrum. Parents will reap what they sow when they continually degrade and humiliate their children. A baseball star who was visiting a prison summed up his success by remarking that he hadn't disappointed his father. One of the prison inmates responded, "I didn't disappoint my father, either."

Those who thought a "retarded" girl was hopeless locked her in a cage to live like an animal. Another person recognized her potential and treated her according to that vision. The "retarded" girl was Anne Sullivan, who later became Helen Keller's teacher.

3. Use your senses—touch, talk, and listen. The power of touch transcends words. One mighty sermon of the Savior wasn't taught in words, but in actions, through the service he performed when washing the feet of his disciples. A picture televised of President Gordon B. Hinckley cradling President Spencer W. Kimball's hand was very touching. That simple gesture conveyed such warmth and caring.

This unspoken, physical communication can many times be the most powerful tool we use with our families. A pat on the back can mean acceptance or praise, and an arm around the shoulder can be sympathy that will be welcomed by the very proudest. Touch is absolutely essential to growth and social response.

Sometimes our "janitorial" duties seem to take our whole

lives. With all the dressing, lacing shoes, buttoning buttons, fixing ponytails, and brushing teeth, we may mutter, "I can't wait until someone around here can do something for himself!" And it *is* wonderful as the children gain a little independence, but there's a special feeling in reaching out to them—literally.

We all probably need to spend more time talking "to" rather than talking "at." It is shocking at first to hear that the average parent really only talks to his child four minutes per day, but this estimate is probably quite realistic. If we could just realize how therapeutic our talk is! Even plants are reported to thrive when talked to. But somehow we find ourselves talking "at" the children—we're always trying to punch in those "teaching moments." We forget that the just plain chit-chat is medicinal. We all have hopes of our teenagers talking to us about their lives—dreams, hopes, fears. But they won't then, unless they do now.

I'll never forget the time I snapped, "What do you want now?" That boy went looking for someone else to listen. Fortunately, his dad had more sense than his mother. We need to learn: think, then speak; listen, don't judge; sympathize, don't give advice. Many times children just need a listening ear.

4. Fill in with supportive influences. We may not be able to afford costly pieces of art, but posters or prints that show positive themes are worth more in the long run. And just because we don't all have libraries in our homes with leather-bound volumes of classics, that's no reason for us to have nothing worthwhile to read. There are magazines, books, and especially Church publications, to fill every shelf and bare spot. The public library costs nothing. You may not be able to expose your children to a symphony (perhaps you wouldn't choose to anyway), but good music is abundant. Once again, your library costs nothing. There's a wide selection today of records and tapes for all ages and they teach positive moral values.

We can't underestimate the power of external influence—and especially that of music. The Scotsman Andrew Fletcher said, "You write the laws, I'll write the music, and I'll rule the country." We have to be careful and watchful at each stage of our children's development. Do the games and toys they receive teach industriousness and integrity, or greed and selfishness? Does their music cause inspiration—or perspiration? Every single thing in the home makes some type of statement to the family. It's up to mother to insure that those deposits into their development banks are worthwhile.

We know that the more positive influences we provide, the less room there will be for negative or even mediocre ones. An accomplished student said that her success was due in part to the fact that as a child she had not been read nursery stories. Instead, she had been exposed to such classics as, "Captain, My Captain." The little verse immediately comes to mind:

> You may have tangible wealth untold,
> Caskets of jewels and coffers of gold.
> But richer than I you can never be—
> I had a mother who read to me.
>
> (Strickland Gillilan)

It's easy to feel guilty on reading that verse—especially if you have a large family. Of course, it's fairly easy with one child. Our first child's constant demands at fifteen months were "dorey, dorey!" He always wanted a story. The value of reading together weighed heavily on me and so I made sure he was read to: in the car, in the foyer, and at the drive-in.

But with a few more years and a house full of preschoolers, the reading moments became less and less. My sense of guilt increased with the thought that I was robbing my other children. But I learned to be realistic. Somewhere along the line as the demands increase, some things will have to give a little. A mother has responsibilities in many areas, not just one. She can't let everything go to rack and ruin while she spends thirty minutes per child every day reading—she may have ten children.

I readjusted. There wasn't as much time for reading, but quality could become more important than quantity. Our oldest boy heard every Little Golden Book ever written; the youngest ones have heard very few of them. But they have had much more of the *Friend,* scripture stories, and as much as they will sit still for of *Little Men* and *Huckleberry Finn.* The kind of exposure sometimes has to become more important than the length. It's interesting that our oldest boy, who had all the exposure, is the one who enjoys reading the least. You don't have to feel guilty just because some other mother is determined that her three-year-old will know how to read. Just do the best you can with the time you have. You won't ruin your child's mental potential just because you are not "reading up with the Joneses." If you can't read to him every day, try to make what reading time you do have full of positive material. Choose things that will reinforce the values you are teaching in other ways.

Public Enemy Number One is undoubtedly the television. This is a shame, because it has more potential for the good of mankind than any other medium. Unfortunately, Satan recognizes the potential there, too. Why else would he use it so cunningly to peddle his wares? It has become largely "his" medium, and yet often we unthinkingly welcome with open arms whatever messages it brings into our homes.

Should we get rid of our televisions? Often we hear people comment that their family has spent several enjoyable months since their TV broke. Why would it have to break first? We should be able to have enough fortitude to turn the dial to "off." If this fortitude is lacking when it comes to television, our families need strict rules.

Too much TV tends to turn people into observers rather than participants in life. We are supposed to be preparing our families for activity. Both boys and girls need to be industrious and full of life to successfully compete and achieve. Television generally does not enhance these qualities. Instead, it makes the children dull. They learn to stare. Their reading skills are less. They will not be as creative.

Like a can opener, a television should be used when it can be of service. It definitely should not be the constant drone in the background of the home—running just for the sake of running—nor should it be a baby-sitter.

Television does not portray realities of life. It makes us all—and particularly children—less sensitive to reality. It minimizes dangers while glamorizing attitudes, behaviors, and life-styles that we know are wrong. It teaches concepts that are in complete opposition to gospel principles. It lies to us—with an aura of truth. There aren't any "freebies" in life. Candies and cereals won't mean friends and good times. Diet drinks won't guarantee trips to Acapulco (too bad!), and toothpastes can't do anything but clean teeth. We—adults—quickly become conditioned by that subtle suggestion process: what hope can we have that children can survive it? That oh-so-quiet (as well as the brazen) conditioning that enters our child via the TV will have to surface. It may be in outlook, behavior, or personality—but surface it will. There's more to it than a little "distortion."

So *think well* about what things go into your home.

5. "Others" are your good right hand. Have you really thought about what a pot of gold there is in your extended family? A grandma can do in a sentence what it takes mother a month to accomplish.

When a letter comes from grandma, a child will sit up and take notice. He believes it when she tells him what a nifty kid he really is. When grandpa calls and tells him a joke, that's the funniest thing in the entire world! Children react with such enthusiasm to grandparents, aunts, and uncles—it's almost like a miracle! These others provide valuable reinforcement for our efforts.

Even though we have never lived close by, our son has a real camaraderie with his grandmother. With the arrival of each letter, he experiences euphoria. He considers her one of his biggest fans, staunchest defenders, and best friends. When a boy receives a letter from that missionary uncle or cousin pointing out the importance of some big decisions coming up, he pays special attention. We said the same thing, but why didn't he act that impressed when *we* said it?

Our second daughter, our faithful rock, was too sick to go to church—several Sundays in a row. Something had to be wrong, for that wasn't like her at all. And being endowed with the usual amount of "down-to-the-last-minute" Sunday morning patience, I demanded, "All right, there's something else bothering you, and I want to know what it is right now!" The poor little thing burst out crying, "It's this *face;* I can't go to church with *this face!*" "That face?" I questioned. That sweet, cheerful, happy little face? No amount of "Your beautiful little face," "Your happy smile," or other encouragements made any dent whatsoever. Only partially appeased, she finalled relented and came with us. But she was still down in the dumps.

It wasn't too long after I mentioned this to my mother that my daughter received a letter. "A letter for *me?* from grandma?" she grinned. The tide was turned, for grandma had told her how appreciated her sweet qualities were, how precious she was to everyone, and what a beautiful little girl she was. Somehow, when grandmas say things, they sound more true! We need all the credibility we can get, and our extended family gives us more than we could hope for.

And how could we ever thank all those teachers who reinforce our efforts? Those who appreciate our children and their goodness and unique qualities bring such blessings to our lives. How special are those teachers who listen for the promptings of the Spirit!

One such teacher called on a Sunday afternoon. She said that following the lesson on prayer, our seven-year-old had stated that Heavenly Father didn't *really* answer prayers. The teacher thought we would want to know about that. How grateful we were for her insight. We didn't have any idea whatsoever that our daughter had had such feelings.

Several weeks earlier our oldest daughter doubled over in great pain. After being ill for several days, she suddenly seemed seriously ill. After she had received a blessing, the pain subsided. But the next day her condition again seemed very serious.

Alarmed, of course, we consulted our doctor. He instructed us to take her directly to the hospital, where we would be met by a surgeon. The waiting physician soon indicated that he felt her appendix had ruptured and immediate surgery was necessary. The surgery was a success, but the doctor admitted his amazement that the appendix had been intact. It had actually been over twenty-four hours since it should have ruptured, and there was little doubt in our minds that it had been her blessing that had kept her from real danger until we could get medical help.

We were so grateful, but our seven-year-old daughter had missed the connection completely. All she saw was that her sister had received a blessing, and still required an operation. Many positive feelings were gleaned from that difficult time, but if it had not been for her teacher's awareness, one little girl would have seen only that Heavenly Father does not really answer prayers!

6. Help your children develop different kinds of talents. I really do think better in Crayola. It's the result of having been through so much construction paper and rubber cement and cardboard. "Providing a wide range of exposure during both early and middle years will guide children toward achievement in life," the inspiring child-rearing books say. More realistically, a child may be guided toward achievement, but mother is being pushed over the brink.

When our first son was small he was my protégé. When I painted, he painted; when I sewed, he had sewing cards; when I cooked, he helped or played with play dough. After all, no stone could remain unturned in helping him prepare for his future role. All in all, it was quite a rewarding experience. But even then, there were occasions that should have been the writing on the wall.

One fall a friend and I decided we would start painting. Of course, we built easels for both children so they could paint right along. Doesn't that sound rewarding? Doesn't it seem like the type of thing that would cement the mother-son relationship?

Wouldn't it help him develop himself? Well, that's what *could* be said, but there surely would be a lot of "pages missing" somewhere.

I could have made him a proposition: "Look, I know you are only three years old. But do you think you could just act twenty-five?" No such luck. He just kept acting like he was three! One morning I left the easel for five minutes and returned to an empty paint tube—Prussian Blue, to be exact. Oh, I found the paint. It was on the walls, the sofa, the carpet. Did you know that one tube of Prussian Blue oil paint has the capacity to cover a whole side of a white frame house? Was I compassionate and understanding? (After all, he needed the exposure.) Will he stand on Mother's Day years from now and remember how his understanding mother channeled his talent? Absolutely not! (Well, it was a learning experience of sorts—he never did it again.)

We want our children to have experiences with different media, but we want them to keep order. They need to experiment in the kitchen, and in the garage, while we need to retain sanity. It's a never-ending circus as they grow.

Somehow our perspective alters as kids come and go. Our first daughter could make crayons appear out of thin air. We decided they were like manna—she kept "finding them on the plain." She did grandiose wall murals for two full years. One night as Dave and I were scrubbing the crayon off a wall I remembered an artistic friend's recollection. She said that while her younger sister had been confining her efforts within the lines of a coloring book, she herself had been coloring free-spiritedly on the walls. We had laughed at the time, but now, as we scrubbed and scoured the evidence of our own "free spirit," it wasn't quite so funny. Do our children really have to drive us insane during the talent crusade?

Grooming talents takes time, it makes messes, and it frays nerves. During those moments we may have to make some personal adjustments. (There's more than one mother who wears earplugs during the hours her children are practicing their musical instruments.) But that exposure to ballet for your awkward little butterball may lead her to greater poise and worthwhile activity later on.

Remember that there are many talents that don't require a class or tuition. Some people equate "developing talent" with "cost per lesson." Our own normal activities can be a training ground for tremendous talents. For instance, we can teach our children to be compassionate and to serve. Assisting us in good deeds is of the greatest importance in their development. True, our compassionate services should be secret to the world, but they can speak loudly and clearly to our families. We can also help our children recognize talents in others: sensitivity, an understanding heart, a listening ear, a cheerful outlook.

A little girl arrived home one day sobbing that all her brothers and sisters had won prizes in the poster contest at school. That meant a roll of tickets to the school carnival for everyone but her. For the others, however, winning was easier; they were artistically inclined. Mother tried to point out some of her talents. Although not quite as visible, they were still valuable. Good qualities are true talents—but it's hard for children to understand that in the beginning. We have to point it out to them.

7. Support your children. A mother's "being there" is irreplaceable at all those wonderful events of childhood—recitals, programs, and so on. But "being there" also means something else. There are times when our children, like us, need to retreat and rejuvenate a little. Those moments are easy to miss, but they are the times we definitely need to "be there."

A teacher called one day to ask if a particular child had come home for lunch. Even though he had packed a sack lunch that day, he had instead come home during his lunch period. His teacher was cross. She reminded me that it was against the rules, that he should know better. What would you do? Sometimes we are too quick to jump to the aid of the "authority" without first investigating the circumstances: "Why didn't you tell your teacher you were coming home? Don't you know the rule about leaving during the day?" Instead, we might try to see it from his point of view. It might just be that he needs to know that mom is always happy to see him. When it's a tough day, and his demands squeeze too tightly, he may need some "space," just as we all do.

Many events occur in our children's world that push them toward home—and mother. Those needs can and should be filled at home, while at the same time we help them deal with their responsibilities. Our children view life very seriously. Their play is their work. There are times when life seems hard and children need someone to put arms around them and understand. As parents, we should be grateful when they come to us. Our emotional "being there" may be just what they need to carry them over at times.

8. Include your children in your life. This can be a hard thing to do. We may easily resent and resist the invasion of what little privacy we claim. It is not difficult to become irritated when a child pipes us with "Who was it?" as we hang up the phone. Yet we frequently do the same thing to our husbands, and we're not trying to be rude or irritating. We merely want to be included. We're interested in what is going on. So are our children.

Sharing possessions can be hard, but sharing ourselves may be even harder. But children want and need to be a part of our peripheral activities. (Other than chores, that is. Hobbies, errands, and shopping are in a different realm than chores.) By including them as they grow, often on a one-to-one basis, we can develop the friendships that will last a lifetime. Even though she was probably murmuring under her breath, my mother endured my being there—and I'm grateful she did. When I ruined her freshly done picture by painting a typical fourth-grade tree smack in the middle, she said it was perfect! Committing ourselves "beyond the call of duty" is hard at times, but it's also right.

Yes, there are exceptions. Children do not need to feel they are welcome to do everything we do or accompany us everywhere, every time. Some parents are guilty in this other direction; they feel their children are as welcome as they are, no matter what the occasion. It just isn't so. How pain-inflicting that attitude can be! How embarrassing (and costly) for mom and dad, and infuriating or distracting to others, when a loose four-year-old overturns a table of ceramics at the arts exhibit! And bringing our toddlers to a musical presentation, for instance, when others have made arrangements for baby-sitting, is not fair to those others. There are areas of propriety and consideration for others that we sometimes breach. There are many events (particularly in the Church) where all family members are welcomed and wanted. But there are also other times (yes, even at church) when events would be appropriate for older children or for adults only. We need to be considerate of others.

9. Learn to relax and enjoy your children. My visiting teachers were tickled one month to see little notes taped around the house that reminded me to "Loosen Up!" For some people, loosening up comes naturally. For others (like me) it involves more effort. But generally we find that, as we grow and learn, we also learn to relax and enjoy our families much more.

Our first baby's bathtime was not at 10:12 A.M.—it was 10:00 *sharp*. The schedule ruled supreme. With the sixth precious one, every moment was sheer delight. Never once was her night waking an inconvenience, for that became the time I could have her all to myself. Suddenly, it didn't seem traumatic that she threw her bowl like a Frisbee and splattered oatmeal in twenty-five directions. Each new experience seemed delightsome. Babies and children are to be cherished. Fortunately, time helps us realize that.

If only we were Polaroids—zzzph! Moments could be captured forever. But, alas, we are not cameras—for us, freezing the joy takes more effort. But it isn't that painful. The first step is to stop, and then look and appreciate. There is such an extraordinary amount of pleasure to be found in a face filled with expectancy on the way to a birthday party, or in hearing a happy little voice call out, "Who wants to play with me today?" The frustrations of a budding seamstress rise to the top like cream, but if we skim below there's that joy of watching her become a woman. That chance may not come again. The "Hey, mom, *I did it!*" look thrown back over the shoulder of the boy whose foot finally connected with the ball might be lost forever if mom had dropped him off and rushed off to her next task. These little things give pleasure to our lives and make many of the menial things more bearable.

If there's one area of life it's easy to rush, it's ball practice. Everyone has to be delivered all at the same time, but to different locations! You know how "idea people" plan the length of that sports season, don't you? They take a "sample mother" and moniter her throughout the weeks of practices and games. When she is on the verge of throwing in the towel en route to the sanitarium, they tack one more week on, and that's it. Slow down, mom, enjoy it.

Slow down? Relax and enjoy? Articles make that sound so easy. How could something sound so easy and be so hard? Because more than in any other area of our lives, "uptight-type" problems come with children. They keep us wound tightly. Some problems will work themselves out with time. Others require more attention and effort. Facing them squarely and dealing with them isn't easy, but it's the only satisfactory solution. A friend's grandmother didn't like passing trucks when she was driving, and so she would just shut her eyes in the process. She caused at least some "near misses," and who is to say how many accidents? With children, we need to keep our eyes wide open and work with them to solve their problems. We can't shut our eyes or ignore their problems, hoping they'll work themselves out. A "near miss" is not an "all's well."

Even with our best effort, there are some problems that are going to take additional attention. This fact doesn't reflect on the "goodness" of the mother, nor does it indicate a "defective" child. It's a natural part of life. This is our growing season.

Some children are quiet, some are studious, and others hang from trees or keep piranhas and tarantulas for pets! There's an endless variety of personalities. Yet it seems we are sent those particular spirits that we're best suited to mother.

Children can frustrate and exhilarate us. They have an innate ability to leave us either tickled pink or stunned speechless with their highs and lows. But in spite of the moments of "It's just not worth it!" or "Aren't they ever going to learn?" or simply "I'm losing my mind!" I still feel such pride as a son grows tall and his challenges prepare him for the priesthood role. I love that little face with the big "root-beers," a freckled nose over that toothless, flashing smile as she dashes out the door in search of a new adventure. I feel such companionship with that straight-arrow daughter, who is so theatrical that she refuses to ride her bike, all because a spider sashayed across the seat—last summer. (Who else could understand her?) Where would my life be without the two boys: One cherublike, cheerful little guy with tiny tennis shoes and a nose covered with angel's kisses; the other, our sweet, sensitive, good citizen with his sense of humor. And then, of course, there is the baby—with curls, bright eyes, and fat little legs that churn away as she jabbers. What a joy! Would I trade it? Would any of us trade it? Not for any price, for our "simple understanding" helps us to know what it's all about, really. That simple understanding is our knowledge that a mother is irreplaceable. Elizabeth Keubler-Ross said: "Each person is like a snowflake: unique, beautiful, and here for such a short time." Our children are our snowflakes.

NINE

EENY, MEENY, MINY, MOE

Hey, Mom! Don't think I'm discouraged, but sometimes these kids don't cooperate the way I thought they would. It's my job to teach them, right? It's their job to listen and learn, right? Then why does it sometimes feel as though it's "them against me"? Don't worry, though. They may be winning some battles, but I'm bound and determined they won't take over the war! Somehow we are all going to emerge victorious! (I hope! Meanwhile, could you pray for me from time to time?)

Albert Schweitzer claimed, "The most successful way to raise children is by example, by example, and by example." Was he correct? Consider: Will children read and learn the scriptures if they never see their father sit and read them? Will they learn the value of prayer without the example of their mother's prayers? Will they learn how to work if their father is lazy? Will they have positive attitudes if their mother is a complainer? Our conclusion is: We will never be better parents than we are people.

We teach and point things out, hoping that our children will understand and follow. But guess what? Once, twice, and three times just won't get the point across. We'll be much better equipped to handle the situation if we realize that in the beginning.

Somehow the necessity of repetition gets underrated. Our job is not over once a lesson is taught. Sometimes we have to "shake it till it's dead." One Mother Education teacher stressed that a child must have eighty repetitions before a principle is engrained. I know sometimes it seems like it's been *at least* eighty times.

It seemed astonishing to me that our Mutual was having a manners dinner to teach youth some of the social graces. But a leader said that when children become teens every lesson they have learned up to that point will have to be repeated. I was deflated realizing a monster of such magnitude was looming on the horizon. With six children, eighty repetitions per child once and then again at puberty—why, that was 160 times per child. Each directive, for instance, "Dirty socks don't go stuffed under the dresser," would have to be repeated 960 times—all at different times and at different stages. Taking a conservative estimate of 200 standard variety lessons of life, that would mean 20,000 repetitions. And can we trust the really important eternal lessons to minimum effort? Of course not, so we'll probably have to double at least half of them. Who would have believed it? Fortunately, there's an amount of "monkey see, monkey do" in our teaching—another reason to set an example for them to live up to.

To complicate matters further, most children have Dr. Jekyll/Mr. Hyde personalities. You think you are going along just fine and then, abracadabra—they are acting very strange indeed! One daughter at age five was so receptive and teachable that we became spoiled and were totally unprepared for her at age seven. It was like a nightmare! What had happened overnight? Why was she acting like that? A standing joke among the adults as we were growing up was, "It's just another little stage!" Having six kids growing in and out of "stages" about every thirty seconds doesn't make life any easier, but recognizing and anticipating this surely does make it more bearable.

We are charged to teach our children correct principles. Unfortunately, that charge doesn't include specific instructions or step-by-step directions. It can present quite a dilemma. There are so many options, and such a limited amount of time! Should the selection of subject matter be left to chance? Should we narrow the field by random selection—eeny, meeny, miny, moe? That doesn't make sense. Obviously, we need to have a goal in mind. And it's going to take consistent work to keep it in sight as we go through the ins and outs and ups and downs of each new stage.

Every field of education has both "required" and "elective" offerings. Because each child is unique, there should be a selection of "electives" to help him become well-rounded. Still, there are certain academic principles that every child should clearly understand. These are the "required" courses.

Teach the Things of the Spirit

Spirituality will be born at home. It is, once again, the example of the parents that shows the true value of this principle as well as how to apply it.

Teach children to pray. A child participates in prayer earlier than in any spiritual activity. Toddlers know to fold their arms, and—other than an occasional morsel hastily stolen to hold them over—they wait until the blessing is offered before eating. But prayer is not only a learning experience for them, it is a teaching technique for us. Even though we are talking directly to our Heavenly Father, we also have a captive audience! Our children need to hear us vocalize our feelings and our dreams for them.

Prayer is a resource always within children's reach. They can understand that at an early age. When our son was terrified before a dental appointment, he asked if we could pray in the car. He wanted Heavenly Father to help him be brave. It was at that moment that the importance of prayer really burned itself into my heart. Why should we be surprised when one little girl, finally responding to fists beating upon the bathroom door, walks out and states quite simply, "I was praying to Heavenly Father because my goldfish is sick." We should have known.

Our kids will sometimes find themselves in tight spots requiring decisions that may be both unpopular and difficult. As they grow older, they will find themselves alone more and more at decision time. We will not always be there to support them—perhaps no one will. But through prayer there will always be a place for them to turn.

Help children understand their relationship to Heavenly Father. Regardless of their age, children can never hear too often, "You are a child of God." We could not overemphasize that our children have a spiritual Father who really and truly cares about them, knows them, and loves them.

"Who loves you?" we ask the tiny ones. Children love that kind of game. Along with the expected responses, "mommy, daddy, grandma," we can remind them repeatedly to include "Heavenly Father" and "Jesus." With those names we give them a tight squeeze and kiss them, reemphasizing in a way they easily understand the warm sensation of being loved. As they grow older, they repeat our simple prayers. They can learn to vocalize the feelings, "I love thee, Heavenly Father."

Soon they will not rely on us. An age comes for every boy and girl when he or she feels that no one really cares. Yet that low point is the time we may actually abandon them spiritually—after all, they seem so grown, so independent. Because their bodies are tall, we think their spirits are tall, as well. But they are still fledglings, stretching their wings. They don't seem to want our care or protection, and it seems hard to offer it, perhaps. But that's the time we need to remind them, again and again, "Hey, someone does understand. You are a child of God. Heavenly Father cares; he will help you."

In our world, where despondent people wander aimlessly (physically or emotionally), there is a great strength in Latter-day Saint children's knowing for a fact that their relationship with their Heavenly Father is real. Knowing they are sons or daughters of God—that they individually were important enough to warrant Christ's sacrifice—will certainly do a great deal in building their self-esteem and confidence to "choose the right." Their attitude is a positive, "I am *somebody*—I am a child of God."

Teach children obedience. Within the gospel framework, it is critical. While worldly schools of thought will contradict one another, for Latter-day Saints there need be no discussion. The fact is obvious: Children must learn to obey.

Obedience for the sake of obedience itself may determine the outcome of weighty matters. "Do it simply because I said so!" isn't necessarily unfair or unjust. Parents should not have to explain the rationale and point out the logic *every* time instructions are given. Elder G. Homer Durham related a perfect example that took place at the time of the Hole-in-the-Rock expedition. Three young children had to be left alone for a time while their parents literally guided their wagon down the two-thousand-foot incline. The baby had been put upon the blanket between the legs of a five-year-old boy, and an older girl placed beside them. They were told not to leave the blanket until their father returned for them. That was the end of the instruction. After the wagon had been lowered and the mother (who had received a serious injury) cared for, the father again climbed to the crest. There he found his children—safe, upon the blanket. Members of my own pioneer family were part of that expedition, and now I wonder: Where would we be today had they not been an obedient people?

Would our children respond immediately to a command that could protect them from potential physical injury? If we directed, "Stand in this spot," would they do it? Would they demand to know why? Even more important than physical safety, however, is eternal safety. The protection they need will come through obedience. Our Heavenly Father gives us many commandments, but the reasoning and rationale are not always clear. The need for obedience is still critical. If it weren't, we would never have received the commandment initially.

How can we expect children to learn to obey the Father they don't see, if they haven't learned to obey the father they do see? There are really only two ways to go in life, and this fact is more evident today than ever before: We will follow the Lord, or we will follow Satan. Every decision our children make points them one way or the other. It is a reality—we must teach them to obey.

Teach children to be reverent. Sometimes we don't give reverence the importance it should have. We marvel when we think of the manner in which the Savior dealt with the many injustices directed at him. He was flogged, spat upon, ridiculed, humiliated, and degraded. But at such times, he consistently remained in control. He taught forgiveness and compassion. The only circumstances in which he became angry came as a result of irreverence.

I wonder what the Lord would say to us should he visit our places of worship. Would he find irreverence "within our temple walls"? It was interesting to read a published letter in which an investigator stated flatly that we Mormons don't appreciate what a beautiful message we have, and that our lack of reverence would keep others from joining the Church. In another instance a missionary received a letter from the girl he had left behind. She said, "Please don't expect me to become a Mormon." Startled by this step in the wrong direction he wrote and asked what had prompted such a statement. Having attended sacrament meeting, she expressed her shock at the confusion she had witnessed. She said that in her church the people were quiet and acted with respect.

Well, we question, what's more important anyway, noise or truth? Isn't it the Spirit that converts? Of course, it should be. However, there are many instances when the Spirit may never have a chance to work because our friends can't get past the level of chaos they may experience in our meetings. Why should we go to all the time, effort, and expense involved in teaching the gospel only to have it canceled out by irreverence? We may take the shuffle for granted, but nonmembers view it more seriously. They may easily conclude that our message could not be important if we, as the members, don't act respectfully. We should do our part to give the Spirit a fighting chance.

As surely as a wallet is taken by a pickpocket, the chance for worship is stolen by an irreverent person. His damage may go beyond the bounds of personal worship, though. One Church custodian presented a lesson where examples of irreverence were displayed: a new piano that should have lasted a lifetime damaged to seem years older, costly drapes sagging and soiled from children running in and out, hymnbooks written on and torn apart, pews scratched and worn from abuse rather than use. Every person in the Church could cite similar examples. Why should we be content with this?

The church building should be a source of pride for each of us. We should respect it and do what we can to keep it in model repair. We should always feel proud to bring our friends there, and we should feel confident that others will conduct themselves appropriately.

The chapel, specifically, should be considered a special place. We shouldn't treat it like just another classroom, and particularly at sacrament meeting. It should not be the place for handing out invitations to parties or food-storage questionnaires, waving and calling greetings, or carrying on varieties of business. It's not the place for breaking up peanut-butter-and-jelly sandwiches and passing bites back and forth to "hold the children over" until dinner. Few children have been lost to starvation during a sacrament meeting.

During a Mother Education lesson, the wife of a stake presidency member stated that their children were never allowed anything—period!—to eat at church after they had passed the toddler stage. Her rationale was that they didn't eat every other hour at home, and she couldn't see any reason why Sunday should be an exception. Many times mothers come to church armed as if marching into battle with diversions, treats, and drinks aimed at helping the children "get through it." While something can be provided in the foyer for the tiny ones, older children can probably get through that hour without bags of cereal or stacks of vanilla wafers.

While it's unrealistic to expect a museumlike silence in the chapel, there's no reason for it to sound like a Persian marketplace either. There's a vast difference between rushing little Neil out every time he whimpers and remaining in the meeting until his howls become deafening and no one can hear what is being said. If children are noisy and cannot be quickly settled, we should take them out of the chapel.

One mother was asked how she and her husband, who was in the bishopric, had successfully taught reverence to their eight children. She responded that she had always insisted they sit together where they could see and hear, and their dad would look down and smile at the children. (Isn't that the way it is? You wrestle—he smiles. Stake conferences are so nice! Dad gets a chance to see what life in church is all about from the mother's seat! No wonder he smiles more broadly from the stand the following Sunday.) These parents treated their family with firmness and reinforced it with kindness.

It isn't impossible to maintain order during our meetings. Difficult, yes. Impossible, no.

Ours is a very busy church. We go there for so many activities besides just Sunday meetings that it becomes a second home. We should be able to feel relaxed there, but there is never an event held at a church building where we should be so "relaxed" that our children are allowed free reign to run wild. Comfortably relaxed is not even near rude or wild.

Family members should be accounted for or controlled until they are old enough that we can trust their behavior. If this trust is abused, they should be taken under our wing again, escorted to and from classes, and so on. Then we can give them some rope. If they don't hang themselves, great. If they tug too tightly, we pull them back for a while.

"Saints alive!"—now *that* is an apt reference to children in church meetings. We have to face it—in church as well as away, kids are kids. But reality doesn't give us reason to make excuses like "it's impossible to keep all these kids quiet. We have a big family." Large family or not, there will always be a controlling force—at home, at school, and at church. If parents are not in control, then children will be.

When the mother of eleven children (all under age thirteen) stopped the car in the parking lot, she looked into the eyes of the oldest boy and said, "The car is your responsibility today." That was it. After locking and shutting the doors, he joined the family in the foyer. Another child took the diaper bags, and another took little ones to get their last drinks (no "in and out" during the meetings). Everyone was responsible for something. Then they sat near the front. No, this isn't a "perfect ending" situation. Most of the children in that family were really full of vinegar, and both mother and dad had their hands full every minute. More than once the mother cried, frustrated. But there she was the next week, trying all over again. The point is that they made the effort to remain in control of their children, restrain them, and teach them. Their view of reverence was that it was *their* family's responsibility to set the example.

It certainly isn't always the larger families who are the culprits. There are some families whose two or three children make noise that far exceeds any amount of confusion made by twelve in other families. And then there are the times when children aren't the guilty parties at all. An article told of a ward's seminary students deciding to start a reverence program. They found their success hampered not by their younger brothers and sisters, or by their friends, but instead by their fathers and mothers giving directions, chit-chatting, and so on. We adults surely can call ourselves to repentance as well.

Reverence is an essential quality of a profitable Sabbath experience. Whether it exists or not will depend on *us*. We can each improve, and we can support the others who are trying to do the same. Yes, there will always be days when our children act like they have all just popped a spring. But there will also always be another week to try over again.

Teach children to work. Probably the amount of work children will do of their own volition would fit in a thimble. And generally, their idea of working hard is our idea of hardly working. Nevertheless, work is an eternal principle. In spite of every argument and means of trickery known to get out of it, we should be determined at all costs that our children learn to work. (We can hope that at some point they will learn to love their work. But don't hope for everything at once—first things first.)

Why work? First, work is therapy in action. The person who doesn't know its full value will find life dull, meaningless, and unrewarding. His chances for success are next to nothing. A survey taken among national achievers found two similarities foremost with each: (1) They had parents who believed in a strong work ethic, and (2) They had had teachers who had been strict and had made them work hard. Work is essential for inspiration, motivation, contribution, or success.

We are all guilty of underestimating our children's capacity to work. A baby can't hit his mouth with a spoon, but he can zero in at two hundred yards on a "crawling critter." It will be both ingested and digested before the mother can rush to rescue her little darling! Children are ready to learn when they are tiny. And we won't be able to make up for lost time, for as they grow nearer to the teens the chances of our being successful become less and less.

Sometimes, during those teen years, all may seem completely lost. Even at best we will be challenged! A boy who is able to run six miles easily each morning suddenly can't possibly walk the length of the driveway to pick up a newspaper. A young man who can press 150 pounds as if they were lettuce leaves cannot lift a trash sack. Kids become blind to dozens of lights left on, doors left open, and food left out—but they have super vision when the last box of Cracker Jack falls behind fifty cans of cling peaches. They are stone deaf when you call them, ask them, or plead with them, yet they have supersensitive hearing when someone outside whispers "movie" or "ice cream."

Of course, there is a logical explanation for these phenomena —the adolescents' bodies are changing. That is the explanation for everything. Even though they can animatedly talk on the phone for hours while doing their homework, it's out of the question for them to talk while putting up dishes or folding clothes. The force of gravity becomes ten times greater than muscle power: That's why the towels never make it back to the towel rack, why clothes are continually piled in heaps, and why their "debris" is never picked up and put away. Excuses double for each year that passes, so it's better to get children trained early.

Some of the hardest work we do is getting our children to work. It will always be easier to "provide for" than to provide "opportunity for." But we see too many examples of failure in instances in which people are "kept" rather than "supervised."

Cain inquired, "Am I my brother's keeper?" We surely should be our brothers' (and our children's) teachers, helpers, inspirations, guides, and supports—but certainly not their "keepers." Examples are all around us of both youth and adults who seem lethargic, have no sense of competition, no zest or "get-up-and-go." But, if they have been "kept" instead of taught, why should they feel otherwise? They never will have had the satisfaction or experienced the increased capacity that comes from challenging work. The loss is theirs and society's. What a waste of talent!

There is a time factor to consider. Our children have very busy lives. Many of them have outside jobs. Most go to seminary, and then there are sports, music, mutual, and school activities. All of these are building blocks for their growth, and we want them to participate. Because of the demands, we may think we are being supportive if we relieve them of home responsibilities. (And besides, all the way around, we would rather just do it ourselves.) But a mother who tries to do everything so her daughter can devote more time to musical talents will find disappointment when the girl is grown and married. There will be a time during that girl's life when there will probably be no piano for her to play. But (like it or not), as a wife and mother, she will have endless bathrooms to clean, beds to make, and meals to prepare. Will she be ready? A boy spared distasteful chores at home will be ill prepared for his work in the "real world." Are his parents really doing him a favor?

The children in one family all recognized their wonderful

mother as they left, one by one, for college and missions. What an exceptional mother she was, and how they all loved her! But what wasn't to love? She did absolutely everything for them. She made no demands on them at all because demands would "interfere" with their childhood. There was no tension at home. All their friends were envious. The kids were all carefree, fun-loving, easygoing people. Life was nirvana as they first left home, but it turned into a hell later on for some of those children—and for the mother in many respects. Some of the children still expected her to fill their every whim. One girl spent years calling her mother every other day to ask, "Mom, how do you cook such and such?" Sons expected their wives to wait on them as their mother had done. It was easier to bring the grandkids to grandma every other day—she wouldn't mind. What a tragic end for a mother who had tried so hard to do so much! In the matter of work, it is not enough to show our children by our example the way to be; we must make sure they have the opportunity for practical application.

The cry goes out from every direction, it seems: Today's kids are under too much stress. If there's excessive pressure, you can bet work isn't the culprit. Work doesn't cause stress—it causes strength. Certainly, children should not "just work" all the time. Balance is just as important in their lives as it is in ours. We can help them learn the principle of having a time and a season for each thing. They are only children once, and they should enjoy it. But they grow quickly into adults, and if they are not prepared, misery is ahead.

No doubt about it, work is hard. But there's nothing wrong with some good, hard knocks. (Rocks put in a tumbler turn into gems—some take longer than others!) Our experiences polish us and give us more competence and confidence. When weighing the pros and cons of an afternoon paper route vs. an early morning one for their son, parents opted for the early one even though is meant much more inconvenience for all of them. Reasons like "But it's just too early" didn't hold water for long.

Soon there would be seminary, then a mission call, where the discipline of early rising would be needed. They felt that if life gets an early start, so should they.

Physical labor is really good for kids, but sometimes it's not an easily accessible commodity. We may have to create our own opportunities for work the best we can. A little boy was struggling to drag out a heavy trash can when a neighbor woman interceded, "Oh, he's too little to be doing that." But his mother expected him to work at it. Not every job is easy, but how many children have died from dragging a trash can out once a week? (Although they will make you *think* they are dying.)

We must pay the price, of course, by getting them started, keeping them going, and following through. No doubt about it, a mother has to be tricky to get kids to work. Our family has had chore wheels, chore boxes, and chore charts—where fish swim, flowers grow, faces smile, spaceships zoom, and eyes peek-a-boo. You name it, we've had it. In the beginning, inventiveness helps. "What will she do to trick me into this? Well, might as well humor her!" It's the result that counts—they learn, and the real payoff is what we're doing for them.

There's not one teenager in a million, however, who will lift a finger to see Jack climb up a beanstalk on the chore chart. Obviously, we have to change tactics as they get older. Then we can rely on rewards and incentives (more commonly known to mothers as bribes and threats). Combined with some imagination, they may do the trick, at least temporarily. It's all temporary: If you think you have stumbled onto a "miracle tonic" because something worked once, you're in for a hard fall. We have to be as resilient as our children are.

A friend and I were both having trouble getting certain of our kids out of bed on time, and nothing short of warfare had really changed things. She proclaimed: "The early bird gets the worm." Soon her children were accumulating little paper grubs each time they were up promptly. So many worms entitled a child to a handsome reward. This sounded good so we gave it a try. Soon

Brad Bluejay, Lisa Lark, Robyn Wren, Brent Bobolink, and Stevie Swallow were counting squigglies. (Put this kind of chart where you don't have to stare at it at dinner.) Cheers! It worked—that time. When I tried it again, they weren't about to fall for it. One summer, to keep them interested and away from the television (with its accompanying cry of "I'm bored!") we read our way to Waterworld. With each book a day of fun got closer and closer. The catch: By the time the "day of fun" arrived, I'd been harassed to the point of reading my way to psychiatric care. Nothing is easy unless you have a family of "vanilla" kids. But we just trudge along, remembering that we're on the upward trail.

Rewards and incentives do play an important part in children's learning the work principle. This is consistent with the gospel plan: We, too, are promised rewards when we are obedient and work hard. Rewards also help children learn to set and meet goals, both short- and long-range. "Payment," however, should not be considered the same as a reward. There's nothing wrong with keeping a jar of dimes or quarters to be paid for extra jobs, but no family member should labor under the illusion that he must be paid for every effort he expends. Every family member has a responsibility to contribute his or her individual best to the well-being of that family.

Teaching children to work eventually operates for your own good as well as theirs. With everyone assigned and doing a share (like it or not), then most of the janitorial chores are done by school time. Allowing another two hours for laundry, cleaning a cabinet or two, and so on, the rest of the day is free. Mother then has control over time; it can work for her. She can read, cook, attend meetings, prepare lessons—even make new chore charts. During the summer months, the children will be up and participating when others are still sitting around in pajamas whining, "Do I *have* to?"

I hate to do things that are beneath me; we all do. Kids are no different. No matter what his age, a child likes to feel that his task is worthy of him. A four-year-old might not be terribly excited about the prospect of cleaning car windows, but with a squirt gun filled with cleaner and a paper towel, he'll probably be squirting every window and door and slick surface for a block. When turning out lights turns into a hassle, an honorary "Light Patrol" responds to the call. (That's a particularly useful ruse. Designate a "Diaper Patrol," and you will never run for another diaper!) The children's enthusiasm diminishes, however, as their age increases, and the honor must continue to meet their age. An eight-year-old Cook of the Week delights in setting the table and peeling carrots, but by the time she's thirteen or fourteen this is no longer true. Her responsibility then will have to be considerably greater if she's still to consider it an "honor."

Everything takes time, and success comes step by step. If the children cooperate, wonderful; if it is fun, all the better; but if not, it is still necessary for them to learn to work. Remember the Chinese proverb: If you give a man a fish you feed him for a day, but if you teach him how to fish, you feed him for a lifetime.

Help your children find enthusiasm in living. Many times over the years different people have asked, "Did you come from an active family?" meaning, of course, "Did you come from an active-in-the-Church family?" I didn't. But did I ever come from an active-in-*life* family! Throughout our early years, it seemed the entire family organization was involved in every conceivable activity. From ceramics to crabbing, we tried most everything. The adults were active and the youngsters were always included and welcome (at least we thought we were). We not only participated in their activities, but they supported ours. Everyone in the clan could be counted on to buy greeting cards and cookies and candy bars and to attend every recital and program. If it captured our interest, it never dawned on us that the other family members might not think it was okay. Although we may have been deprived in those early years in terms of Church exposure, we were rich in one of life's valuable commodities—enthusiasm.

The word *enthusiasm* comes from the Greek word meaning "god within." And it can make the difference between a plain "vanilla" person and one that is "tutti-frutti" all over. With a healthy portion of it and a good attitude a person has a much better chance to arrive victorious at life's end. Compare him to those who drag along and can't for the life of them see above the soles of their shoes.

The day-to-day demands of motherhood can get to us. Sometimes we seem to forget the real frailties of our small charges. Due to circumstances beyond our control, the value of helping them build enthusiasm may become blurred. And, of course, we cannot teach what we are not. In urgency or bewilderment, mothers have the sad ability to squash the beautiful, naturally endowed spark. They can kill their children's enjoyment for life. This treasure by Jill Sparger sadly depicts "The Tragedy":

> I always wanted a red balloon,
> It only cost a dime,
> But Ma said it was risky,
> They broke so quickly,
> And besides, she didn't have time;
> And even if she did, she didn't
> Think they were worth a dime.
> We lived on a farm, and I only went
> To one circus and fair,
> And all the balloons I ever saw
> Were there.
> There were yellow ones and blue ones,
> But the kind I liked the best
> Were red, and I don't see why
> She couldn't have stopped and said
> That maybe I could have one—
> But she didn't. I suppose that now
> You can buy them anywheres,
> And that they still sell red ones
> At circuses and fairs.
> I got a little money saved; I got a lot of time;
> I got no one to tell me how to spend my dime;
> Plenty of balloons—but somehow
> There's something died inside of me,
> And I don't want one—now.

These words often ring in a mother's ears: no time, not worth it, too risky, too expensive. Each is a killer phrase that unfortunately destroys more than just the pressure of the moment. It destroys something very precious and worthwhile—that natural sparkle. What a force of righteousness and productivity our youth could be in life with the "I can!" "I am!" attitude.

Momentary pressures often carry a lot of clout. Consider how easy, for instance, it is for us to squelch our children's enthusiasm if we ourselves are suffering from the H.A.G.S. (Husband Always Gone Syndrome). When suffering from this affliction, it's hard enough to maintain a level attitude for yourself, much less work with the children. We've all had it from time to time, in varying degrees.

After Dave blessed our second baby a friend exclaimed, "Was that your husband? I thought you were a widow." He had been gone almost three weeks of each month during our year in that ward. But even in the best of times, somehow the daddy is mysteriously called away right at the critical moments when you need him the most. From sudden hospitalizations to parades, he will be gone.

And does he ever attend those carnivals or back-to-school nights? It was during one of those that I was momentarily captivated by a teacher's abundance of niceties. (We all bask in those moments to the point that we become slightly intoxicated and forget to conduct the every-two-minute head count.) Suddenly, rrrrrrrng! went the fire alarm. The bell was clanging, people filing out of the building, and who do you think was standing wide-eyed by the alarm handle? (He's a sweet, obedient, and charming child. But what chance do I have of convincing those who witnessed the scene?) "Where is his dad when I need him?" I moaned.

One day a friend and I decided (admittedly, in a moment of weakness) that after Primary we would gather our kids and take them to an exciting restaurant. It was Halloween, and the restaurant was offering a free meal to any child in full costume. No typical Latter-day Saint mother of many can resist such a temptation. The "spot" had a seating capacity of two thousand. It was one of those rare and charming places that cause a loss of

91

reality (as well as sense of direction). There were mountains and caverns and waterfalls, terraces, trails, pools, patios, shops, and arcades. In a word—it was *terrific*. (Oh, by the way, did I fail to mention that our husbands were out of town?) Yes, the fear of natural consequence should certainly have been enough to pulverize our enthusiasm—two women with twelve children all costumed to look like the other fifteen hundred children present. Ever tried to hang on to one small clown in a sea of small clowns? But if we hadn't plunged right in with enthusiasm, a rare moment would have been missed. (Fortunately, those "rare moments" don't happen too often in one lifetime.)

A real enthusiasm-squasher is a flat, dogmatic statement like "Forget it—it costs too much." We don't want to crush the kids—even if they ought to forget it and it *does* cost too much. True, children do have to learn financial reality—it seems that they always want everything and generally have a minute understanding of the value of money. Our reaction, however, makes a loud statement to our families.

Two mothers, of equal means, respond to a request from their children. One says immediately, point-blank: "We can't afford that, it costs too much. Besides, it's not worth it." The second mother stays calm. She asks questions about the request. If at all possible she tries to help the child find a solution (perhaps a way to earn the amount) or a compromise ("If you earn half, I'll be good for the other half"). At the very least, she gives a considerate explanation that it will simply have to wait. While the first mother's reaction pushes children into thinking of themselves as "poor," the second mother at least tries to help them learn to solve or to understand financial dilemmas.

"Working it out" can mean entirely different things in different circumstances. The children of one family wanted a new swing set, but it was out of the question at that time. Instead of saying, "Forget it!" the mother put the question to the children, and they decided they would at least try to earn the money. They sold homemade bread and donated their own allowances. Everyone was required to sacrifice. For some that meant giving up hot lunch at school, for others it meant drinking powdered milk instead of dairy milk, and there were no family home evening excursions. The money was pooled into a community pot. It was a lesson in tenacity, and they bought the swing set.

Not every family is so lucky, however. The three little girls in a second family wanted a playhouse. In their situation, however, it wasn't just a matter of "tightening the belt." Their family belt was on the last notch. They were already drinking powdered milk to save money, their lunches were simple and always packed at home, family home evening treats like movies came once a year if at all. All "extras" had long since been given up out of necessity, and there was no reserve from which to pull. Still, it was the mother's attitude that determined the outcome. The sweet mother in this particular family was blessed with a rare disposition. Her solution to the playhouse problem was really basic —a refrigerator box cut and decorated. She did the best she could with what she had instead of saying, "Forget it, it costs too much."

Children naturally anticipate anything that requires special notation on the calendar—Arbor Day, St. Patrick's Day, Eat Pork Day, just anything! If mother anticipates their excitement and goes along with it (as cheerfully as possible), they are on the enthusiasm trail. They will think you are Numero Uno when you serve hamburgers and french fries for April Fool's Day breakfast, and will leap off into the day like they've been set on fire!

Everything turned red, white, and blue during the American Bicentennial year. It was hard *not* to catch the spirit! People were painting mailboxes and water hydrants, stitching quilts, and collecting all sorts of memorabilia. (We even had our own Bicentennial baby—since we'd collected just about everything else to mark that landmark.) About midway through the year a friend and I came across a bolt of Bicentennial T-shirt fabric. We burst out laughing and for two days sewing machines whirred constantly. The morning of the third day dawned to find eight children identically clad in patriotic shirts and blue shorts. The summer's uniform was established. It was a great year for many reasons, but when the older ones come across pictures, they laugh and remember their American shirts. These silly things are the happy memories children keep close to their hearts. They are the things that will push children into their own family traditions. They'll do such things because they remember and know it will be worth the effort.

That's enthusiasm—give a good, strong dose of it to your family for their own good! Our daughter Lisa won a turkey at Thanksgiving one year, and when someone asked her how she'd done it, she said, "Well, I just *really* wanted that turkey, so I just *tried*." A lot of people never try to win at life, and with that attitude of never trying, they never will win. Let's kindle a fire of enthusiasm within our youngsters. The blaze will undoubtedly smolder at times, but it will burst into a flame of activity somewhere along the way.

Teach Children to Honor Their Mother

Forget dad momentarily. Why? Because mothers generally are already very conscientious in teaching children about their father's contribution. In more cases than not, women go to great efforts to reinforce in children the idea of what a special dad they have. Mothers, however, don't do too much of this for themselves. After all, that's so "self-centered." Ideally, the father should be the one to emphasize the mother's role, but in reality, it often gets pushed into the background. Although a child instinctively loves his mother, he must learn to honor her. He must be taught that she is more than someone to wait upon the family, fix meals, and clean house.

The young years are busy years for all of us. There are so many habits, traits, and values to teach. We work and work to help mold our children so they will be equipped to make decisions for themselves. It's important to us that they contribute both to society and to the Church. We are anxious about their exaltation. Isn't all that enough to worry about?

The Savior instructed us to be servants—not slaves. We have to be the ones to teach our children how to help themselves, and then let them do it. If that lesson isn't learned, mother may find herself living in what one woman affectionately refers to as the "burnt toast syndrome." Somehow stories always come out on Mother's Day about how wonderful mother was merely because she always ate the burnt toast. In the long run, how much will it really be worth for family members to remember mother as the one who could be counted on to eat what was left? After maturing, they will undoubtedly come to realize that it was a selfless act on her part. But during the "together as a family" years, children may easily think, "Well, it doesn't matter—she likes burnt toast." If mom gets what's left over, what no one else wanted, what does that say for her?

Many future adults will probably look back on Mother's Days and recall how their mother would never have ice cream when there wasn't quite enough. But wouldn't it be better for mother to take a very small, token portion, requiring a small amount of individual sacrifice from each child? It would require little effort, but would reinforce the idea that mother is a person of at least equal status as other family members. It's not that mother needs the ice cream; it's that the children need to give it.

This advice from a little grandmother-type woman was given sweetly, but with authority: "My dear, you must learn that you are the queen of this home. Your children expect you to do the things they are fully capable of doing for themselves." It was food for thought. If we do "too much," or do things that the family should be doing for themselves, things that are important for their growth, then we actually are robbing them. With "too much" we encourage leaning instead of standing, selfishness and ingratitude instead of serving and thankfulness. "Too much" makes it easy for a child to become a "taker" in a society where there are far too few "givers." A queen of a home will serve her family, while helping them to be capable themselves. Children must be taught to recognize their mother's value and to honor her properly. Sometimes we need to remind ourselves of that same thing.

TEN

TO ACT OR TO REACT—THAT IS THE QUESTION

Dear Mom: I don't know how it all really happened. there were screams and shouting. The first one yelled; the second one jerked. He said, then I said; he was smart to me, so I showed him. This went on until I'd lost any possibility of ever regaining my sanity. I don't know what I'm going to do now, because by the time it was over I'd grounded the whole bunch for the rest of their lives. I'm not sure who got punished—them, or me.

To expect to raise a family without conflict is naive. To expect that "our children will be different" is even more naive. And to expect that bringing up children will be easy is hilarious. Somewhere along the path we will definitely have to deal with the matter of "cease and desist—or else!"

Our need to discipline always arrives before we have developed the maturity to do it wisely. But if we wait, it will be too late! In the world, the subject is either oversimplified or overly complicated, and never geared for those with our particular insight as Latter-day Saints. To complicate matters further, we know our children are more than biological by-products: They are personalities of eternal worth. Therefore, we can't rely on worldly professionalism to teach us.

The scriptures and prophets offer some guidelines. We know

we should reprove with kindness. We should teach correct principles and let children govern themselves. King Benjamin, however, instructed parents that they shouldn't allow their children to quarrel or fight (Mosiah 4:14). And the Doctrine and Covenants warns us that the sin will be upon our heads if we are negligent (D&C 68:25). Even though we are well intentioned, we can become confused in direction. The responsibilities of parental stewardship can stretch us tighter than a bow string, and we become practically frantic to do the right thing. There are many times when we are entirely too rigid, and just as many when we're not nearly rigid enough! In self-defense, many parents defend their methods of discipline as the *only* correct or workable methods. That "golden mean" has not yet been found, and we wonder if things will ever fall into place.

Like most mothers, I've read umpteen books and columns on disciplinary schools of thought. But I finally came to realize that it's the guidance of the Holy Ghost that will best direct us. That guidance will not only point the right way, but the Lord's methods will be consistent with our needs. As we struggle to keep in balance, be flexible, and be teachable, the right combinations for us will come if we discipline by the Spirit.

My husband and I spent many frustrating hours over several years trying to keep children in their beds at night. We obviously have Ishmael somewhere in our genealogy, for we have a family of night "wanderers." And all those books and columns warned that children should sleep in their beds and never with their parents. Around and around we went. It was a stake president, the father of seven, who brought us around. He recalled how he had explained to the visiting authority who was their house guest that a small boy might be found crawling up in bed during the night for a little closeness. That simple incident poured insight. The Spirit simultaneously twisted both our hearts. It was His guidance that would show the right way.

When our most trying daughter made her next attempt to "climb in," we put our arms around her. And it wasn't too long before she quit coming to our bed. Somehow during her active life she hadn't been getting quite the amount of closeness that her little spirit required, and during the night she would come seeking. It was merely a temporary need. The expert opinion brought us pain, confusion, and guilt. But since we listened to the Spirit, life has been a hundred percent more pleasant for all.

Expert opinion may abound, but the scriptures are the best text. We all marvel at the people continually referred to as "stiffnecked." How could they have been so blind? we wonder. But could we share that label? It seems that many times we are equally unyielding and unbendable. Certainly there are rules of order that children must learn at an early age. They must learn to conform to certain patterns of behavior: They don't walk on furniture, use the cat for a football, and so on. And there are spiritual laws, too, that demand obedience. But sometimes the children are not the ones at fault.

During disagreements do we hang this motto upon our hearts: "I'm the mother. I'm going to have the last word, and that's *that!*"? In order to be victorious in that philosophy, we pour salt, and then more salt, into the wounds of our children. One day, as two of our boys were engaged in a growing argument, I appealed to the older one, "Please, please don't make an enemy of your brother. He wants to love you. Don't make it hard for him." How quickly I forgot those very words. Only hours later that same boy and I were going the rounds, and I was bound and determined to win. After all, there was the cardinal rule of motherhood to uphold: "The mother should always be right." After observing our bitter words and injured feelings, my husband, without knowing the events of that morning, quietly said to me, "Don't make an enemy of your son." Stiffneckedness! It brings heartbreak.

Ponder the questions Alma asks:

> Behold, *are ye stripped of pride?* I say unto you, if ye are not ye are not prepared to meet God. Behold ye must prepare quickly; for the kingdom of heaven is soon at hand, and such an one hath not eternal life.

> Behold, I say, *is there one among you who is not*
> *stripped of envy?* I say unto you that such an one is not
> prepared; and I would that he should prepare quickly, for
> the hour is close at hand, and he knoweth not when the
> time shall come; for such an one is not found guiltless.
> And again I say unto you, *is there one among you that*
> *doth make a mock of his brother,* or that *heapeth upon him*
> *persecutions?* Wo unto such an one, for he is not prepared,
> and the time is at hand that he must repent or he cannot
> be saved! (Alma 5:28-31; italics added.)

What is the extent of our own pride, envy, and the manner in which we may ridicule or persecute even our own children? Surely we can see that it would be much more desirable to bend, apologize, and ask forgiveness. "I'm sorry; I had no right to talk to you like that. Will you forgive me?" These words will help us win in the relationship, not lose. We certainly don't want to make enemies of our children. We don't want them to view us as their persecutors. We need to relax, loosen up, and remember that losing some of the battles may help us to win the crucial war.

In a desperate attempt to regain control, every mother has succumbed to the temptation to warn, "If you don't . . . then you can just . . ." We have to be careful when using a threat technique, for we'll never win unless we're completely prepared to follow through. A mother who had simply reached the end of her rope with her teenaged son's table manners finally gave him the ultimatum. He could clean up his act or he could eat in the garage with the dog. The boy must have eaten in the garage for two years!

We have to remember that we are the adults and they are the children! Kids *should* act like kids. Sometimes we worry too much that our kids aren't acting like adults, when what we undoubtedly should be worrying about are the adults who are acting more like children! Line upon line they learn. And in all fairness, can we realistically expect more from our children than we are willing to give? Discipline shouldn't be a case of "do as I say, not as I do."

Sometimes we offer excuses for ourselves in self-defense. The bedtime hour is the most critical and trying part of my day. I used to say, as though it justified my actions, "My patience is unlimited until 7:00 P.M. Then, look out! It's the Wicked Witch of the West! That's just the way it is!" But I've learned that that isn't "just the way" it should be! How can we expect our children to develop any amount of self-discipline if we rely on "cop-outs" too? We each have to learn self-mastery.

Our self-mastery helps us maintain the capacity for spiritual reception. Dissension is Satan's tool. Unfortunately, however, children soon learn it is a major tool of the power play in the social world. They see that arguments lead to victory in playground squabbles. Children are bright, and will figure out that if dissension is effective there, it will also be effective at home. They will think that if they can reduce us to the level of argument, there will be at least a possibility that they can control the moment.

We should refuse to argue with our children. We can offer them sympathy, assistance, firmness, or discipline, but still refuse to argue with them. This way, we will leave the confrontation satisfied. At least we will have kept the channel open for the inspiration to do what's right. "And now come, saith the Lord, *by the Spirit* . . . and let us reason together, that ye may understand" (D&C 50:10).

ELEVEN

THE MERRY HEART HAS A CONTINUAL FEAST

Dear Mom: This point in time will appropriately be dubbed the "Dial-a-Dispensation." We can dial-a-lash, dial-a-prayer, or dial-a-date. Why, we can even dial-a-day. Sure enough. It can be milk and honey flowing when set for "dial-a-good-one." But if it's set on "dial-a-dud," it can sure turn sour.

Life can seem as complicated as a Chinese puzzle. The further we get into it, the easier it seems to get stuck somewhere in-between. Once down, there's no better time for deep-breathing exercises. (Deep-breathing exercises are supposed to help us better handle our stress.) But careful not to poke your head down in the smog. Make sure you get a good, strong whiff of the right attitude.

As the puzzle pieces of our lives pile upon us relentlessly, our reactions are normal: "Help! I wasn't trained to handle this!" During those frustrating times, the little thought creeps into mind, "A cheerful heart and smiling face pour sunshine in the darkest place."

Does attitude really count more than aptitude? Absolutely! During our Air Force years we met a young woman who was quite remarkable. While everyone else was moving around "putt-

putt," she was "whizzing." What made her unique? She had only one arm. Physically she had a handicap, but emotionally she held a firm grip. A positive attitude and some perseverance can be the key ingredients for turning your particular lemon into lemonade.

There's always a choice: We can whine, or try to win. Songs like "Born to Lose" weren't meant for us—those are swan songs. We have an eternal perspective, and an inheritance from our Father. We have the power in us—to win! Once the wheels are set in motion, we find attitude and enthusiasm can't be confined. They pour over into other areas of our lives. Enthusiasm breeds more enthusiasm. Suddenly, we find we're not just enthusiastic about the possibilities of our roles, but about the challenges as well, and then about our Church assignments, and then about personal activities. We can make it happen, but as the saying goes, "If it is to be, it is up to me."

We have to get ourselves together. In other words, we must work on getting and maintaining a top-notch (meaning healthy, not vain) self-image. It's the most important piece in the puzzle of a good attitude. A woman with a suffering self-image won't be able to appreciate her own worth, interact socially, or communicate with her husband or family. She'll become ineffective in other capacities.

Your self-image will be positive to the degree that you do what is right. It has been true forever and will still be true when the sun is cold: Right is right no matter how many tell you it's wrong, and wrong is wrong no matter how many tell you it's right. There's nothing that can put a bounce in your step, a sparkle in your eye, or confidence in the way you look at yourself the way a clear conscience can. The statement made by President Harold B. Lee to youth certainly applies to us all: "Be loyal to the royal in you."

There's a fatal disease that can't be treated by medicine— negativism. Like the proverbial albatross around the neck, it can truly become a heavy burden. Dump it! If your friends are continually morose and unwilling to try to see a bright side—dump them! If this seems extreme, remember that if you allow others continually to unload on you, you will soon find yourself turning into a garbage can of negativism. We can make choices when it comes to our friends. And for those casual acquaintances with whom you must work, try to (1) rub off on them, or (2) keep your chin up and endure. Be cheerful and optimistic, and find friends who are the same. Offense is our best defense. Catch those others ("Boy, it's a great day for cleaning the chicken coop!") before they have a chance to get to you ("Ugh, gotta go drag through that filthy mess—*kerplunk!*").

We can all learn a lesson from "Dee-dee Merriheart." That's not her real name, but it should be. She's never failed to at least try to pick out the bright side. And sometimes it has been trying. Her fun-loving husband loves to "surprise" her, and she never knows what will be next. When he brought silkworms home to raise, she was calm, even though they soon had infiltrated all the draperies. Her outlook was healthy as she watched her long-anticipated sofa torn asunder—how else could all the little gerbils be found? I probably would have said "toss them" if my husband had waltzed in late one night with a hundred pounds of potatoes that demanded immediate attention. But she was still laughing and having a good time after midnight as we all sat in the bathroom peeling a tubful of potatoes. (See, it's catching—she had us doing *her* potatoes!) Yes, "Dee-dee Merriheart" has a great attitude. And it was only with her that I volunteered for a camping trip even with a week-old baby because I knew it would be fun. (It rained for four days, not one fish was caught, the tents leaked, the car broke, and we all—kids, parents, and dogs—had the most marvelous time imaginable.)

Some of life's challenges are definitely more enjoyable than others. But get as enthusiastic as you possibly can about each. It may be a lot more exciting to think about making a new dress or buying a chair than about painting the outside trim or cleaning the basement. Nevertheless, those things have to be done anyway. Make the best of it.

We all have to live with limitations. But we can learn to do the very best we can within our range of resources. The fact that there are barriers doesn't mean that prospects are nil. Too often we find people who squash their possibilities before they ever start, simply over money. A woman provided some lovely table decorations for a luncheon. As everyone admired them, another woman snapped, "Well, with all her money she can afford to do it that way." She needed to look again, for there wasn't a costly thing there, except maybe thought and effort. That price may be too high for some.

One convert, the wife of a prominent professional man, remarked that they had found life much harder among their ward members as he became more successful. The more money they made, the more estranged they seemed to become. As medical students they had been cheerfully recognized by others as "struggling peers," but that changed with their success. She seemed to be the same friendly, talented woman she had always been. She worked very hard at her Church callings as well as in the community. But suddenly, because she had money, her efforts became appreciated only in terms of how much she may have spent.

This negativism can also be quietly engendered in our children, hampering their future success. Do they wear shirts, for instance, that read "The Devil Made Me Do It," "Hell on Wheels," or "The Bad Apple"? Why not "The Apple of My Daddy's Eye," "You Make Me Smile," "Face It—I'm Lovable!" or "Specialty of the House." If they must be labeled, let's at least give them labels to live up to. (Well, once I was tempted by a shirt that said, "One Kid for Rent—Cheap.")

The saying, "You can't teach an old dog new tricks," is fine if you happen to be a dog. But as daughters of God, we know we have the ability to change and make ourselves better. Our innate resources were not created just to be wasted. Nevertheless the spirit within us testifies that these words I have seen attributed to Oliver Wendell Holmes are true: "The average man goes to his grave with his music still in him." And this is kindred to the words of John Greenleaf Whittier:

> Of all sad words of tongue or pen,
> The saddest are these: "It might have been."

So let's take a firm hold on life and move forward in only positive directions. We can be happy, thin, successful mothers, good teachers, or anything—if we recognize our unlimited potential. Be realistic, decide on the path, be willing to pay a price to get there—and you will.

TWELVE

THE HOME IS ALSO A HOUSE

Dear Mom: Remember when we read Gone with the Wind? *How I dreamed of living in a house just like Twelve Oaks with winding staircases and rooms that went on forever? Whew! I'm surely glad that wish didn't come true, because I'd be cleaning forty-eight hours a day! (Can you imagine the garden?)*

How flimsy a "house" really is—just brick and board and nail! It could be gone in a moment's blast. But "home"—that's something else again! It should be a place of strength and security. It makes sense that we must build our *homes* with sturdier stuff than goes into building a *house.*

Our homes should be constructed with righteousness. There should be peace, an inviting warmth for all who pass by, and an atmosphere of respect for individuals. Home should be filled with sweet sounds of music, and, of course, laughter. There should be rich, warm fragrances that only a mother can provide —breads, cookies, and hearty meals that fill more than empty stomachs.

In our small temporal capacities, we try to build in some qualities of heaven. Would our Heavenly Father live in confusion and disarray? No. Our homes then, should be clean and orderly. Would he frantically try to maintain his authority? No. Likewise, our homes should have discipline as well as love. Home is where two people who love and respect each other share a mutual goal of exaltation, where they lead by their example those spirits they have been blessed to bear. It's a place of education for everyone and growth for all. It is where love offers security and protection for children. It is where we teach them blessings of work, and where we work out our own salvation. It's the island for a family in life's turbulent seas. A place of contentment and fulfillment—this is home.

However, a home is also a "house." The rooms may resemble the Black Hole of Calcutta, closets in reality may seem more like death traps, and windows may attract every particle of soil for two square miles. No matter how spiritual we are or how lofty our ideals, there are still groceries to be purchased, clothes to be washed, and weeds to be pulled. These are the realities of a home. If we're going to be happy or successful, we must deal with them professionally.

Clean Up Your Act

There really is happiness to be found in our own backyard, but not if we trip over the rake looking for it. Generally, the degree of satisfaction we find at home will be about the same as the degree of order we keep there. Heavenly Father is a God of order; he is organized. We inherited from him the ability to thrive under orderly conditions. Amen to the comment, "I don't work well spiritually if my physical life is cluttered."

The Church is not made of perfect people. (If we were perfect, we wouldn't need the Church.) It's a tool that helps us learn principles that prepare us for godhood. One of those principles is order. We can't be called failures just because there is some room for improvement in our lives. But many times we react as though we had no hope of succeeding.

It never fails: During those Relief Society lessons where meaty discussions could be centered around ways to improve, people become defensive. Instead of discovering ways to be better, we are reduced to defending the way we are. Should we be ashamed

107

if we're not perfect? Absolutely not—but we should be ashamed if we are not willing to try to improve.

"Clean it up" lessons are very much like thin ice—we tread carefully. No one wants to say anything that would be hurtful to another. Out of basic consideration we may make excuses for others (as well as ourselves). When visiting teaching, have you ever been greeted by, "Oh, just ignore the mess." What should we do? We could just say nothing and go on pleasantly with our visit. But instead, we reply with something ridiculous like, "Oh, don't worry about it. You can't do any better with your big family." Or we say, "Well, you can't do everything. The mess will still be here tomorrow." (Part of that statement is true, anyway.)

Frankly, no matter how we love that woman, it's next to impossible to "just ignore the mess." Piles of laundry, stacks of dirty dishes, and a stench in the nostril are hard to miss. It's difficult, no matter how we love children, to welcome into our arms a crusty-nosed toddler. Matted hair and soggy diapers hanging do not encourage open arms. It's not that we wouldn't like to overlook these things if possible. But it isn't something people still in our state of imperfection can simply "just ignore."

There is the fact, too, that not everyone loves us. We open our doors to many others, and greeted by such a display they can't help but be unimpressed. The fact that we've been immersed all morning in Chopin or Spiritual Living lesson preparations won't matter if they have to trip over the vacuum and wonder where to sit. What it *will* say is that *Mormon women are sloppy.* Remember, the rest of the world views the Church by the one Latter-day Saint they know.

Excuses won't alter the facts. People are neither stupid nor blind. We all have days when we get "caught"—that's to be expected occasionally. After all, we have to live in our homes. Children should play, not just sit. A certain amount of clutter accompanies life, particularly during mealtimes, after-school rushes, and times when the traffic is heavy (weekends). There is an obvious difference, however, between this clean clutter and accumulated crud. And we are kidding no one but ourselves if we think that difference isn't apparent.

We have a cold, hard fact to face: *For the most part we are where we want to be.* There will always be a controlling force. If it isn't peace, it will be contention. If it isn't consideration, it will be selfishness. If it isn't organization and management, it will be confusion and chaos. We hear repeatedly (and perhaps have said it ourselves), "Well, I can't help it," or "What in the world am I supposed to do with this family, church, school, and all?" or "I'm just a step ahead of disaster." Realistically, this is the type of excuse we would expect to hear from one of our children. We can never feel whole or healthy if we are the victims of our homes instead of the masters. Our children will never catch the vision, or achieve, without an example. There is a lot more at stake than simply a clean house.

Church assignments, too, are no excuse. If our husbands performed their professional tasks the way we sometimes perform our homemaking tasks, there wouldn't be food on the table. Church assignments don't excuse a man from reporting to work on time and finishing projects. This isn't what the gospel teaches. Our Heavenly Father doesn't expect us to live our probation a step ahead of disaster. He has intentionally endowed us with the ability to control the elements around us. Surely, he expects us to do so.

Master, or Martyr?

Within the little kingdom of our home is an area I "lovingly" refer to as "janitorial services." They are as constant as the rising sun. Besides our peripheral activities, we are greeted continually by floors to be scrubbed and toilets to be cleaned. There are the clothes to be washed and ironed and smelly tennis shoes to be aerated. In the refrigerator there's always going to be a little something or other wrapped in foil that does its darndest to mold and smell up everything else. Dried crusts of peanut-butter-and-jelly sandwiches will mysteriously work their way out of the kitchen and find a home under some unsuspecting chair. From our kids there's a constant chorus of, "Who, *me?* How should I know who put that waffle behind the sofa!" And there's the ever popular, "I didn't do it."

It's curious that even with children who are always reluctant to change their clothes, there seems to be a never-ending mountain of wash to be done. And food to prepare. "Hey, mom, when are you going to the store? There's nothing to eat." There's no new twist when it comes to the state of their rooms: "Don't *touch* my room—I know *just where* everything is." Who are they trying to kid? Ali Baba's treasure could be buried six inches underneath that debris, and they'd never know it.

Oh, well, circumstances such as these are standard operating procedure where there are children. But whether these circumstances rule us or we rule them is exclusively up to us. It's a wise bride who, appraising her new home, realizes that the responsibility of its upkeep is now hers. Whether it runs like a finely tuned machine, comes apart at the seams, or falls somewhere in between will not depend on circumstances. It won't depend on her ability to make excuses. It will depend on her taking control.

One year we lived near to "generic" neighbors: two women, same age, same number of children, similar income level, living side by side in twin houses. But that was where the similarity ended. The first lived in such a state of confusion that her home continually had an odor of stale food. The children were always disheveled, and were never seen in clean, well-fitting clothing except on Sundays. Although there was plenty to do, she was bored and unhappy. She was a wreck physically, was a mastermind at excuses, and claimed defensively that she was under entirely too much "stress." The second was always neat as a pin, as was her family. Her home was efficiently run and inviting. She was energetic and lived with a full calendar. It was really quite an interesting comparison living close by but observing them from afar, and did I ever learn from both!

Was Woman One "bored with nothing to do," or was she really disinterested? Was her problem really stress? We truly do work better under stress; it's the *distress* that causes problems. Those stresses that push us forward to meet challenges and get things done are a blessing. They help us progress. *Distress* is a result of losing control. It's not healthy, but it doesn't strike at random, either. It can be prevented—but it's up to us.

Starting Point—"Do It!"

Perhaps my enthusiasm makes up to some degree for my ignorance. Or perhaps my priesthood leaders have the same attitude we sometimes use on our children: "Now just *stay* there until you do it right!" At any rate over the years I've spent considerable time involved in the Inservice and Teacher Development areas. One sad thing I've found is that there are a great many people who would much rather be entertained than taught. But the gospel was not intended to be static; it is meant to be alive and active. The axiom "Do it!" is a perfect motto for each of us.

It almost always takes less time to get something done than it takes to get around to it. Life would be much easier if we could all learn that lesson. One morning I watched a child go to more trouble trying to cram a pair of dirty Levi's into an empty peanut can than it would have taken to drive to the store for a new pair.

Growing up in south Texas was great, except for one thing. The climate was *hot*. And because of the heat, the northern grasses did not grow well. Consequently, the yards were covered with carpet grass. Other than harboring chiggers by the billions, its most distressing feature is that leggy grass runners shoot straight up out of it. The result is a lumpy, loopy-looking lawn. As children, our standing summer chore was: "Cut a bucketful of runners every day." Now, this was not impossible or even difficult (chimpanzee labor, actually: clip and drop, clip and drop for twenty minutes or so). But it was amazing how that assignment triggered our imaginations and inventiveness.

Every day we marched out to fill the token bucketful. And every day we devised an entirely new way to get out of it altogether. Many times we just got lazy and merely tried to pull the wool over mother's eyes. There were endless ways we could make her think we had finished the job. We'd fill the bucket with dirt, over which we sprinkled a paltry amount of runners. Then we'd wonder how she caught on as two of us would drag the "clippings" for inspection. We punched holes in the bucket, "lost" the bucket, and swore a dog ran away with the bucket. As a last resort we clobbered each other with the bucket.

We weren't very smart. Mom would send us out in the cool of the day and we would scheme and plot to get out of doing a half-hour's worth of work. We should have figured it out in a hurry, for when it became the heat of the day (pant, pant), there we were—still clipping runners. And she wasn't compassionate or understanding, either. She would say, "It is good for you to sweat. It will make you healthy."

The analogy comparing work with eating an elephant is true. We can ponder, fret, and worry forever. But taking a bite at one end and heading toward the other end, one bite at a time, will get the job done. Sometimes, as in the case of clipping runners, we have to learn the hard way—but we do learn.

Imitation truly is the highest form of flattery, and one of the most effective ways of being successful is watching others. A Mother Education teacher said that once married she realized she didn't have the slightest idea of how to care for her home. Her own mother, she admitted, had been very loving but not very well organized. There had always been the scurry to "get things decent" before the front door could be opened. The teacher wanted better, but didn't know which way to turn. So she went to the obvious resource—the women in her ward. She noticed one who was good at one thing, and another who was good at something else. She became the student and tried this way and that way until she formed her own way. She now has a well-run, efficient home, full of capable, well-trained children.

Look around. There are people around who shine in efficiency and time management. There are some others who are exceptional in child development. Some are money managers; others are gardeners. Seek advice from those who can help you grow. But choose people in whom you have faith. At a seminar presented by a man who taught time management to corporations, we were disillusioned. The man earned his living teaching personnel to become more productive through proper time management. But we noticed his tie was crooked and his shirt haphazardly ironed. His presentation did not make a favorable impression as he repeatedly had to have additional handouts collated. It might have been just "one of those days" for him (we all have them). Yet, bit by bit, we became more skeptical about the validity of the material itself.

There are as many different ways to effectively manage a home as there are individuals. We find disciples of one formula, and followers of another. One good way isn't necessarily the best way for all. We can adapt various methods that fit our needs and individual circumstances. The important thing is that *something* works well. There is an amount of trial and error, to be sure, but don't be shy about learning (or sharing). Role models abound! "Try on" what works for others and see if it "fits" for you.

Proceed with Caution—Snares Abound

Snares of the "in-between" are easy to get into, but frustrating to free ourselves of. Consider these three:

1. "Fill that model role." I grew up in an inactive family, and so when I married I became a little overenthusiastic about being one of those mythical M&M's ("Model Mormons"). I tried everything that I thought would be typical of a good Latter-day Saint mother—canning, baking, quilting, gluten making . . . there's a myriad of "desirable" talents.

Being able to cook, sew, and take care of a home was fine, but Sister So-and-So could knit! No respectable Latter-day Saint wife could go through life without knitting. So I bought the books and materials and asked instructions from anyone who would answer. Subsequently I produced two ski sweaters for my husband (he was so impressed), an afghan for grandma (she was just tickled), a cabled coat for mom (what an accomplishment), and a couple of baby sweaters (no explanation required). And that was absolutely *the end* of a budding knitting career. In short, I *hate* to knit! I never liked it. It made me tense, and I could think of at least ten thousand things to do to make better use of my time. The motivation had been all wrong. Learning simply for the sake of learning was pushed aside by my trying to fit the "model" role.

A lesson became crystallized through all those miles of yarn: Learn for the value of learning, but don't try to be someone you are not. In each case the saying is true: "When they made me, they broke the mold." We each have our own "mold" to perfect. Although we should be interested in gaining as much knowledge and experience as possible, we won't be able to fill someone else's mold.

2. "Competition is healthy." There are times in every woman's life that she lets herself slip into competing with other women. Yes, there may be a form of "healthy" competition, but this type is "unhealthy" for sure.

While grocery shopping may not be listed among the most thrilling activities in life, still, it isn't the worst, either. There was a period, however, when I actually avoided the grocery store during the five o'clock rush—not because it was busy, but because that was when the "working women" came in to "pick up a few things." They looked so chic—from tweed coordinates to attaches. Their purses didn't say "Baby's Stuff" or "Taxi Driver," but "lizard" or "alligator." Of course, they really didn't all look as though they had just stepped from the cover of a fashion magazine. My perspective was way off center.

A hard second look made me realize I didn't need to stand behind the beach-ball display until they were gone. No, I wasn't dressed in a smashing suit, but I was wearing pressed slacks and neat blouse (usually maternity). My hair was fashionable and my makeup fresh. Why should I hide in shame? I hadn't been caught barefooted and wearing holey or faded jeans. I didn't have chipped fingernails, hair in rollers, or a face that hadn't seen makeup in over a month! I was dressed appropriately for my pro-fession—homemaker. I was dressed appropriately for the task at hand—buying lettuce and trash bags. Our life-styles were merely different.

We should improve for the sake of improving, and not because of feelings of inferiority or intimidation. We're all valuable, talented, and interesting people in our own right.

3. "It's just not fair." An interesting aspect of our job as homemakers is that we are called upon to do a variety of things for which we aren't trained or qualified (or in which we aren't even remotely interested). We waste a lot of valuable time wailing, "It's not *fair!*"

Let's consider one of our profession's "occupational hazards." (Job descriptions downplay those activities.) Camping, for instance. A job description may state, "some camping required," but it would never mention the three days of prepara-tion, the filth, inconvenience, vermin, rotten quarters, or foul weather—much less the six days of repair time found in the after-math!

My idea of camping is going to the Holiday Inn in some mountain community. Unfortunately (for me), the real benefits for a family that come from camping experiences can't be found at the Holiday Inn. (This really isn't a very smart example, because it will probably end up underlined in red and left on my pillow.) Oh well, I *like* sleeping in a leaky eight-by-ten-foot tent with six kids and a six-foot, five-inch husband all packed in like sardines. (I'm the one on the air mattress that always deflates around 2:30 A.M.—just in time for a nocturnal boulder to make its way up through the earth and position itself exactly between my shoulder blades.) The children can't understand why it's only when camping that mom is up calling, "Come on, it's a great day! Get up, everyone!" at four-thirty in the morning! No job in the world is easy, sometimes it isn't pleasant, but whether it's "fair" or not ranks "0" on the scale (1 to 10) of importance.

Those Four-Letter Words

"Four-letter words" are usually considered undesirable vocabulary. But there are two that are treasures: *time* and *work*. The implementation of these two can produce dramatic things in our lives.

Brigham Young was known to lay it on the line when teaching principles of the kingdom to the Saints. He advised them not to ask the Lord to do what they were not willing to do themselves. In Proverbs 6:6 the admonition to work is put even more succinctly: "Go to the ant, thou sluggard; consider her ways, and be wise." But President David O. McKay stated it beautifully: "Let us realize that the privilege to work is a gift, that power to work is a blessing, and that love of work is success." (Quoted in Richard L. Evans, *Richard Evans' Quote Book* [Salt Lake City: Publishers Press, 1971], page 46.)

You Spend Time, or It Spends You

Some "labels" make us bristle slightly (companion, chauffeur, cook). But there's one label often included in those lists that is a real claim to fame. That is "efficiency expert" or "time manager." A woman efficient in time management is ambitious and her enthusiasm serves her. She's the master, not the victim.

We live in a wonderful age. There are times when living with our conveniences seems to inflict guilt on some. I'm not sure why, but we've all known women who want to "do it just like grandma did." Perhaps grandma's struggle to maintain the status quo brings us guilt when we consider the ease of our duties. When the air conditioning broke during the heat of the summer, one sister said, "We don't need it. The pioneers did just fine without cooling." Certainly, we can survive—but is the fact that our ancestors didn't have something any reason for us to refuse it? That's like refusing to take the plane simply because grandma had to walk.

Our times are different; our challenges are different. Our pioneer mothers' lives revolved around the mechanics of staying alive—eating, cleaning, maintaining. Today, we are freed from most of their wearying and time-consuming activities. Surely the Lord expects us to use this blessing to our best advantage. Twenty-four hours today are the same as twenty-four hours a hundred years ago. The time passes as predictably as it has always done. But our options for ways to fill those hours are not nearly the same. We can spend that time, or it will spend us.

The benefits of efficient home management today are two-fold: (1) the good it does for us personally, and (2) the way it serves as a means to an end. We are in control. Good management allows us time and energy for families, Church assignments, and the particular requirements of this dispensation, such as genealogical work. Our grandmothers and their mothers could never have devoted as much time to genealogical research and temple work, for instance. Even if they had had at their disposal the technology, they did not have the extra time required. Their time was used mostly in the regular course of living. Where much is given, much is expected.

Multiple Choice: Plan or Fail

Work won't be as hard if it's well planned. But we simply won't get anywhere if we don't know where we are heading and have some idea of how to get there. If our route is not well mapped, we will probably end up on a side road, sidetracked and very possibly over the edge. The first question we should ask ourselves is, "Where do I want to go?" (or what do I want to accomplish), and the second, "How do I get there from here?"

The passage of time does not work miracles. Too many people fall into the trap of thinking: "When we are through with school . . . ," "When our children are grown . . . ," "When we are out of debt . . ." The plain truth, however, is that time will not do one thing—but pass! Another common misguided thought is that someone else "has more time" than we do. Wrong again. We all have varying circumstances. Some have the ability to use their time (much like the flow of a waterfall is harnessed into electricity). Others sigh and sit in amazement while watching the view.

Keep Your Feet on the Ground

Be realistic when setting goals for yourself—especially considering the range of difficulty. Make it believable *and* achievable. Then boost yourself and tackle something more challenging.

A friend and I overestimated our capabilities at the outset of a building project. The result was that we came very close to severing a hand with a circular saw. What we should have done was recognize our limitations and take the time to seek the advice of a more informed person. Get help if you need it. Remember that success breeds success, and by the mile it's a trial, but by the inch it's a cinch.

How long will that project *really* take? Being basically impulsive, I have been a long time learning this lesson. But I'm slowly being tempered by the realization that everything is going to take about four times longer than initially planned. We have to set limits, or time goals, for our work. Some projects could be drawn out forever. But unless you have unlimited time (which you don't) adopt the philosophy "It doesn't take long to do nothing." Push to work at the maximum speed (particularly when doing the mundane) at which you can still achieve quality results. No time is saved if the chore has to be done twice. Challenge yourself, work fast, and do the job right the first time.

Evaluate your goals in terms of time and cost. Ask at the beginning of a project, "Am I following this plan out of love or necessity?" If the answer is love, then take as long as you like, perhaps spending more for the item than you would if you bought it already made. View the endeavor as a creative experience. However, if the answer if necessity, there's an entirely different measuring rod. In sewing, for instance, firm believers in the axiom "sewing is cheaper" may be kidding themselves. Sometimes, yes; always, no. Cost per yard for fabric is only the tip of the iceberg. "Hidden costs" (for notions, patterns, trims, facings, and linings) have skyrocketed since I learned to sew. Those considerations will multiply the total price for a garment four or even five times. And time is worth a lot, too. If a garment can be made for twelve dollars that would cost sixteen dollars in a store, you have saved four dollars. However, if that project took a good chunk of time that was needed somewhere else, more was lost than gained.

Additionally, the saying, "You get what you pay for," should be considered. We need to cut corners where we can, but the little outfit we "whipped up for a song" will be worthless if it has to be washed down the drain the next day due to poor quality materials. Don't trip over a dollar to pick up a dime.

Another measuring rod for value: Do you like it—or not? There are times when a bargain is no bargain at all. As children grow, we all know, they develop definite tastes. It won't do any good to come home with a bargain if no one will wear it because they all hate the style.

Taste is an important aspect in our planning. The time saved by cooking the whole month's main dishes in one afternoon can be a lot. However, if no one in the family likes the changed consistency of the food that has been frozen and reheated, what is that saved time worth? Why spend hours weeding rutabagas and beets if your children hate them? Weeding time should be worthwhile; grow what you will eat. Don't rob your hard work by poor planning.

Outcome Is Set by Input

The initial plunge is the hardest part of swimming, and the first step is the hardest part of any job. Success requires more than token effort. We have to jump in and get stroking.

Part of our problem is that we're spoiled. So many of the normal tasks we do require practically no effort whatsoever.

119

When we're thirsty a twist of the wrist brings water—but anyone who has primed a water pump can attest that it can take quite a lot of effort to quench a thirst. And even though the pumping becomes easier after the initial price is paid, it will still require attention to continue the flow. A self-motivated person is becoming more of a rarity. But he is still an asset wherever he's found. That successful individual who looks so cool and "in control" is really more like a duck—calm and placid on top, but paddling like crazy underneath.

Habit Shows the Real You

Time is precious. The way we use it will send us on our own particular way. There's a song that says, "When you choose the very first step on the road, you also choose the last." Our first step should be carefully weighed; it's the choice in our beginning, but also the choice of our ending.

President David O. McKay said that the real calibre of a man could be measured by the types of thoughts he had when he didn't have to think. Our real character likewise is exposed by our choice of diversion as well as occupation. How we use our "free time" especially tells a lot about us. It is said that we build our character from the bricks of habit we pile up day by day. The irony is that it takes such a long time to develop good habits, and such a short time to develop bad ones.

We have to use our time constructively if we are to build ourselves for eternity. Today's technology has produced devices that better all mankind. But many times we either abuse them or simply don't use them correctly. Consider the telephone. Excessive telephone "chit-chat" can be a sure disaster to a woman. But those who are "hooked" could at least find constructive activities to do while talking (ironing, laundry, and so on). Then they would be less likely to turn around at the end of the day and find that the most productive time has passed. Remember, though, that a chore done while talking to a friend will probably take twice as long. A phone is fine for talking, but it doesn't help working. (The key: Does something serve us or does it enslave us?)

Public Enemy Number One is *still* the television. Its too frequent or too casual use is a bad habit for a woman. Research shows that TV has the capacity to turn our children into dulled observers. But it also can push us into a state of listlessness, discontent, and disenchantment. Of course, our daily schedules are not like menus that read "No Substitutions!" If we're in control, occasional television watching is fine. But if it's a habit, substitute. Get a hobby, read a book, teach someone how to bake bread, take a class.

Remember how hard it is to establish a good habit, yet how easy to form a bad one? Consider that in evaluating how easy it is to simply turn the set off, then keep it off for a couple of days. Are there "withdrawal" pains? That tells a lot. It constantly amazes me to hear the question, "When is there time to read?" A better question might be, "When is there time for television?" It's a matter of personal choice, then conditioning.

For mother there's an even uglier head hiding behind too much television. It can truly be a disaster to time management. And it can be a real threat to both personality and spiritual efficiency as well. There are exceptions, of course, but generally the offerings on public networks (and specifically the "soaps") could be summed up in a word—*rags*. Without being defensive, let's evaluate. Are they virtuous or lovely? Do they teach correct decision making or positive social values? Or are they mainly examples of greed, infidelity, lust, or perversion? They can be particularly insulting to womanhood, and the themes found often completely contradict the gospel principles we testify that we believe and uphold.

Even many Latter-day Saint women spend hours a day with their schedules (their "professional" time) revolving around when "my show is on." When I was visiting an out-of-state friend, I heard her visiting teacher comment, "I don't have to rush now. We bought a video recorder, and now we tape my soap while I'm gone." How are this woman's priorities set? As we weigh the amount of time spent in this pastime, let's consider the familiar verse by Alexander Pope:

> Vice is a monster of so frightful mien,
> As to be hated needs but to be seen;
> Yet seen too oft, familiar with her face,
> We first endure, then pity, then embrace.
>
> *(Essay on Man)*

Remember, whatever goes into our lives will come out. Too much of this type of "input" will result in any number of outputs—all negative. We are not receptacles for the swill or the sewer. *We* choose how to spend our time.

A popular song of years ago advises: "Wake up, wake up, you sleepyhead! Get up, get up, get out of bed!" Is that ever a good habit! Truer words were never spoken than these: An ounce of morning is worth a pound of afternoon. But it won't matter what a morning is worth if nothing is done with it.

Getting up is not enough; it's getting going that counts. A woman who considers her homemaking as a profession will get up early, dress completely (including hair and makeup), make the bed, and straighten the room. Then she can turn out the light and leave that room for the day. Once dressed for the job, there's no reason to backtrack—it's full steam ahead! We act the way we're dressed, and if mother is still wearing her robe after breakfast, she might as well have stayed in bed, for all practical purposes. Other than throwing some breakfast on the table, she probably will not have done too much anyway. A lot of valuable time has slipped through her fingers—the best time of the day. Race cars won't place well if the drivers have had to pull into the pit stop at every pass to refuel or readjust. If the car is fueled and ready when the flag goes down, however, the maximum amount of ground will be covered. Mother, you're the driver.

Work Smart—Not Hard

There's a paradox in the little saying, "The hurrier I go, the behinder I get." We've all experienced it personally at one time

122

or other, and we witness it regularly: A woman hurries and scurries from this to that and yet never has anything done. She's continually doing laundry, but there's always a stack on the floor or the sofa. She's always in the process of cleaning, but the permanent home for the vacuum is the middle of the family room floor. Her home almost always looks like a cyclone just hit. The poor thing is always on the verge of exhaustion and yet can't ever see enough success to give her a feeling of accomplishment. There's only despair and frustration.

Why take all day to accomplish the amount of work that should require two or three hours? It doesn't make much sense. No one could love janitorial work *that* much. (There's only so much satisfaction to be gained from running a garbage disposal and cleaning the lint traps!) Now, there's absolutely nothing wrong with hard work. The hard work that shouldn't be hard is the problem. Don't just work hard—work smart. Yes, we could make furniture polish by boiling linseed oil and whatever else it is that you boil, and we could wax the floor with starch water left from making gluten. But that's not smart—only hard.

Plan chores to work for you, not against you. They should run simultaneously, one just a little ahead of the other. That way ten jobs can be completed in the time it would take for three back-to-back. Having a few good materials is a lot smarter than trying to have a different product for every job. At least fifty pages could be devoted to ways of working smart vs. working hard, but let's just say that it can change your life's work.

Workshops, books, and other sources all offer a myriad of information on the "how to." But the important thing is the "decide to." It will save hours and hours, giving you hours and hours of time to spend more creatively and effectively. Use your head, and it will save your feet.

Bend a Little

A member of a scheduling class voiced the fear that following a routine would make her too rigid. She might become obsessed with cleaning her house. The teacher's laughing reply was, "Fat chance!" That kind of fear shouldn't ever stand in the way of our organizing ourselves. However, the house is not a "sacred cow." It should be organized for *our* benefit, not for the sake of the house itself. Any woman who is obsessed with love of ritualistic cleaning has tunnel vision. (Don't worry if you think you might be one of them. There are only three still alive, and they are at the Smithsonian—relics.)

Even in the most well-managed home there will be a certain amount of "clean clutter"—toys and materials that accumulate during the course of playing and working. However, those things should only take a few minutes and minimum effort to clear. The walls won't crumble nor will anyone die of shock if the schedule is locked in a closet once in a while. The sun may not shine so brightly tomorrow; the floors can wait a day.

A rare showing of a private European art collection was held briefly in Denver one summer. The chance to see it probably wouldn't have come again in a lifetime for most people. Would it make any sense to miss it because it came on baking day (dad could bring home some bread), or wash day (children can wear jeans an extra day)? At the first available moment, half a dozen of us dropped what we were doing, dropped off our children, and away we went. The schedules got tossed in the closet that day. But we came out ahead in the long run because of the lift that comes with variety. "Sorry, honey, about waffles for dinner, but we had a date with Rembrandt!" Why feel guilty? More importantly, why stay home?

Use the Tools of Your Trade

The home is our professional workplace. It should be treated as such. There's a lot of wisdom in the saying, "Make do with what you have," but it certainly isn't very smart to make it our life's motto when efficiency is concerned.

Does an architect go to his office and draw up plans using a folded piece of cardboard for a straight edge? Of course not. He uses a ruler or T-square because he knows that possessing the tools of his trade is essential for quality work. Men have a much more realistic appreciation of the motto, "the right tool for the right job," than do women. To them, having the correct tool isn't a luxury, it's a necessity. (You might notice that it's only in families in which the wife cuts the lawn that there's a push mower parked in the garage instead of a power mower.)

If a man needs to hammer some nails, but there's no hammer, what does he do? He goes immediately and buys a hammer (usually a good-quality one). *Sometimes,* if the job is a one-shot affair, he might borrow one. But what do we women do? Do we buy a hammer? No, indeed, we take off a shoe and pound the nail in with it! We've all done it, every last one of us.

Granted, there are times when making do works just fine. Occasionally hammering some nails with a shoe might fit in that category. But if we're going to do a professional job in our homes, we need the correct tools of our trade—we can't forever make do without them. That doesn't mean, of course, that we have to own every device and gadget known to man. Many people get less done with more things. Simplify, and get the highest quality, most versatile equipment you can afford. It's our attitude of being *cheap,* not provident, that keeps us continually rationalizing, "Oh, I can get by."

Not every mother needs an electric wheat grinder, particularly if her friend next door owns one. Perhaps she uses only thirty pounds of wheat per year. But the mother of a large family who makes homemade bread two or three times a week needs a grinder—it's a tool of her trade. She needs it more than the family needs a camper! She probably needs it more than the dad needs a radial arm saw! Every mother needs an efficient sewing machine as much as she needs a range or a washer. A crepe maker or wok would be nice, but we can probably live quite well without them. However, we shouldn't be trying to sew or cut hair with the same scissors the children bring home from school, nor should we think a twelve-year-old broom will do a sterling job. And how can we expect to keep a clean house with a World War II vacuum relic held together by strapping tape? As we evaluate our individual situations, we can see which items are most used and needed and thus should be considered our "professional tools."

There's an intriguing phenomenon found in many homes: furniture—or more aptly put, no furniture. Let's look again at that professional man. Would a doctor open his practice expecting patients to sit on telephone books? Would an accountant— or an attorney? Realistically, how much return business can he expect if he's always having to entertain clients in an empty office? He may not be able to afford what he would really like, but there must at least be "adequate" accommodations. And, a significant point, will he feel *satisfied* in his profession without them? Yet how many women go for many years without any furniture whatsoever in their front rooms, and a bare minimum in the rest of the house?

Of course, we have to be realistic, too. Our priorities have to be kept correctly positioned. Latter-day Saints marry at a relatively early age, and almost always when there are still the considerations of educational expenses. And because we know the wisdom of having mother in the home and not delaying children "until we can afford it" (we'd be as old as Abraham and Sarah if we did!) there are greatly increased family expenses to be weighed against one stretched income.

We do have to put a top priority on the things that will support our husband's earning ability. Even a higher priority is placed on contributions we make to the Church. And so we weigh very carefully our essential needs (rent, groceries, insurance) against our wants (furniture, landscaping, hobbies). It's reasonable that many (and probably most) times furniture and related things must fall down on the list of priorities. When necessary, this is fine for a while. I suppose most Latter-day Saint couples have lived for at least several years under those conditions.

The problem is that too many times those "temporary" circumstances become the permanent condition. As time goes on, those needs may be kept low on the list of priorities because there is always something "more important" ahead. And, of course, this is considered by many to be part of the "sacrifice" that is essential to righteousness.

One aspect of the problem is also that the husband gets used to not seeing anything in the living room or upon the walls. He may then fail to recognize furnishings as a priority at all. Everything seems to be going along fine: Wife is happy, children are growing, food is on the table (there is always a table).

He really isn't Silas Marner. The wife is not Pathetic Pauline. But if home is to be our profession, then it needs to be more than just the workplace. Mothers are not merely cookers of the corn and sweepers of the floor; they are supposed to be makers of the home. Doing *only* janitorial duties makes a woman regard herself literally as just the "janitor." She has an inherent need to create an atmosphere in the home and to take pleasure in it. If she can't, she will have a hard time functioning efficiently.

A home is not just a place to be, or to clean; it is an emotional island for the family. That is the difference between housekeeping and homemaking. To feel complete in her profession, a woman needs to rest her eyes upon uplifting and pleasant things. They do not need to be extravagant, or even fashionable. No doubt most of us will have to compromise, but we should at least be working on it. Furniture should be on the list of "active" priorities.

Every family should be in the process of creating a home where efficiency works and the mother feels happy. In our present culture a woman ought to be able to invite her visiting teachers or neighbors to sit down in the living room before her children are in high school.

Time Is Money

We once knew a girl who was obsessed with "waste not, want not" when it came to time. If stopped at an intersection, she would quickly hop out of the car and pick up any litter lying about. Then into the car she hopped, and zoom!—off she went. Perhaps she was a little eccentric, but she certainly knew the value of a second. Of course, that's extreme. We want to use time effectively, but we don't want to go through life like a wind-up toy with a battery that never runs down. Who wants to "beat the clock" only to die of exhaustion?

"In this class, we don't deal with minutes, we work in seconds. If we worry about seconds, the minutes will take care of themselves," was the philosophy of a teacher at Brigham Young University. I don't recall most of the Genetics, Medieval Literature, or Church History I studied, but the lesson learned in her business class was worth every cent of the tuition. We all have ambitions and dreams for our lives. Taking care of seconds will allow us the minutes to blend those dreams into the reality of each day.

In our days are tucked here and there available moments that can be put to good use. One such example! A friend has a little motto hanging in her kitchen that reads, "If a woman's place is in the home, they why am I always in the car?" Just think of all the conference talks, music, scriptures, or motivational tapes we could listen to while running our errands. That time in the car could then work *for* us.

Because there's always something demanding our attention, we may have to alter a bit! When inquiring about an advertisement, I laughed at the woman who asked immediately, "Can you hold for a minute?" After a little adjustment she returned with the explanation, "There, I had to lock myself in the pantry to get some quiet!" And I thought only Latter-day Saint mothers had to lock themselves in closets. (When we were given the admonition to go to our closets and pray, the Lord was probably anticipating the conditions of our hectic lives.)

Making a house into a home takes effort. Attending to the needs of the house itself takes effort. That effort is demanding as well as constant, but remember: Eternity is made up of the todays of our lives.

> Look to this day!
> For it is life, the very Life of Life.

In its brief course lie all the
Verities and realities of your existence:
    The bliss of growth,
    The glory of action,
    The splendor of beauty.
For yesterday is but a dream,
And tomorrow is only a vision:
But today well lived makes
Every yesterday a dream of happiness,
And every tomorrow a vision of hope.
Look well therefore to this day!

(Sanskrit saying)

THIRTEEN

DO KIDS REALLY
EAT ASPARAGUS?

Dear Mom: Remember when I would bang my fist on the table and declare that when I grew up we would have cold enchilada sandwiches for breakfast and corned beef and cabbage at least once a week? (If my husband didn't like it he would just have to eat at "the club"!) Oh, that it were that simple!

With the passing of a few married years, things do take on new twists. This is never more real than in the kitchen, for there's usually an added dimension that could tarnish the glitter of even Camelot—the patter of little feet. As to that, some mothers will tell you how their children just loved egg foo yung and liver with onions from infancy, but, don't believe it—they're just trying to intimidate you. Somewhere out there at least one child is bound to like nutritious, well-balanced meals. There must be some here and there who appreciate variety. But, by and large, the only common ground of agreement regarding food is this: Kids want it; mother fixes it.

In the beginning, that little precious one will try to flatter and appease you by hastily gobbling almost anything that rests upon a spoon, accentuating his enthusiasm with a broad grin. But he's just biding his time. One day soon he will emerge like a sultan from the East, demanding this and rejecting that. And don't think for a minute that he doesn't know who has the upper hand.

You can't force him to eat one thing he doesn't want; his jaw can clamp down tighter than a vise at the mention of, for example, turnip greens. He can't be enticed by flimsy promises, either: "Eat your spinach and you'll be like Popeye." (Who wants to look like Popeye?) Nor can he be bribed, and certainly not humiliated: "Heber, please eat. Just think of all the starving children in Timbuktu who would be grateful for a lovely bowl of okra." "Name *one,*" challenges Heber (I'm with him). Of course, it would be silly to say all children are tablewise tyrants, but there are at least several in every large family.

It really doesn't require a psychic to interpret the Mealtime Mystery Game. There is a very basic rule of thumb: Kids like pizza, tacos, or food that comes (plain) on a bun. If it has green things, red things, crunchy things, or is mixed up—forget it!

One day the moment of truth arrives and we mothers realize how intimidated we have become. We wake up to find ourselves putting meals on the table that in yesteryear we wouldn't even have considered meals. What happened to those years when breakfasts consisted of omelettes and muffins, lunch sacks held cold chicken and tarts, and dinners were feasts to the eye as well as the palate? More importantly, what happened to the pleasure that came in preparing such meals? How could we have slipped into "dull and dingy" without really noticing it? It's elementary— we were outsmarted.

Yes, a child may be short, but he is dumb like a fox! Children are not sure of everything they *do* like, but they have very definite ideas about what they *don't* like. And they instinctively know what methods will work best on mother. Again, we are faced with the age-old question: "Who is in charge here?"

I admit that there are some women who simply couldn't care less about any activity that takes place in a kitchen. But for most, losing control and authority in their kitchen is like robbing a dog of its bone—snarl and growl! Even during medieval times the keys to the larder were a woman's badge of honor.

The fact that we spend more of our married life in the kitchen than anywhere else makes it a critical place. It is our bailiwick. Consider how many thousands of meals are prepared over twenty-five to thirty years; the figure is ominous. And the prospect of thousands of pleasureless hours "by command only" can be absolutely debilitating.

And talk about *dull!* Years of nothing but "chicky noo-noo" soup and peanut-butter sandwiches can get *boring*. In all fairness, there's bound to be a minimal amount of variety. Sample five kids sitting around a lunch table. You'll find the first will order peanut butter and honey on whole wheat, the second wants raspberry jam and nothing on a hot-dog bun, the third wants peanut butter and jelly on soda crackers, and the fourth wants only crackers. The last one merely wants a spoon heaped with peanut butter (into which he will push the "noo-noos"). Who says mealtime can become boring?

We want to serve our children's wants. When it is reasonable we cater to their little whims. But any activity that requires twenty or thirty thousand hours of one's life should also be creative, pleasurable, and challenging. (We'll only spend around fifteen hundred hours in sacrament meetings during that amount of time.) If children are harassing their mother into something less, it's time for her to come to a screeching halt and firmly state, "No more!"

Mealtime should be an event, not a circus. Children's lives are regulated by rules, and mealtime should be no exception. It shouldn't be a time for rudeness or free-for-all. Lay down your laws and become a staunch defender of the rules. There's no reason for them to be too restrictive or unreasonable, of course, but without some kind of rules the mother of an active family will surely go mad. We will be tried and tested again and again. But that still doesn't give children license to disrupt the entire event of mealtime.

So the rule is established: No dessert without finishing dinner. This sounds easy enough, but there will always be at least one child who feels he should be the exception. We must stick to the rule and flatly refuse to become a sparring partner: "Too bad, you know the rule, no dessert. See you after the dishes." That's hardly cruel or unusual punishment.

Now, it would be nice to say at this point that it won't be long until they all obey and gobble up their dinners. But it doesn't always work this way. There are children who willingly obey, and some who merely submit. But there are also others who will challenge until the night before they leave for their missions.

If mealtime is successful, it won't be by accident. Yes, here are those principles again: *attitude* and *preparation*. (Truth is eternal.) Our dinner hour will most often be the result of what we put into it.

It would really be hard for even the best of us to get terribly excited about a dinner that had been mentally nonexistent a half hour before. *Problem:* It's late. What about dinner? *Solution:* Quick, fry a pound of frozen hamburger, add some macaroni, and throw in a can of tomato sauce. Open a can of fruit cocktail and warm up some green peas. (Sound familiar?) Toss it on a naked table with some forks, and what a scene! Better yet, kill several birds with one stone. Reach for the tuna. (Some disciples of tuna defend that it was really this versatile fish that served to feed the five thousand.) A single can can be stretched to feed eighty-five people, and there's always enough left over to last another six days. To call this type of meal unexciting is to say the very least.

The frustration and frenzy (and boredom) many times associated with such meals can be cut down by about 80 percent when we spend an hour or two just one day a month planning the menus. The ease of preparation and shopping can also be increased with this method. Pick up calendar. Pick up pencil. Turn on brain. It is more simplified the more explicit we are: days marked when dad will be gone (hot dogs that night, right, mom?), nights requiring late dinners or cold dinners, and so on. Listing the treats for family home evening and lunchboxes also eases headaches. And as long as we're writing, it only takes an extra three minutes to plan a little variety in the breakfast items. This variety takes only a small amount of thought, but it greatly minimizes the probability of daily assaults: "Old oatmeal and toast, as *always,* I see," or "*Eggs!* You never, *never* fix anything I like!"

After you have made a list of main dishes, salads, vegetables, breads, and desserts, meal planning becomes a matter of filling in the blanks. Every family is different, of course, and it wouldn't do you any good to plan meals that would please my family. Still, there's a wide range of possibilities for every family. There's no reason for us to view the kitchen as K.P.

The view of the entire elephant may sicken us slightly, but the first couple of bites we can handle. The month first needs to be broken into weeks. The week isn't too difficult to tackle. For example, there can be a day assigned for chicken, hamburger, a meatless meal, ethnic food, and so on. If everyone's crazy about pizza, you may want to have a standing pizza night every week. And four days per month of chicken doesn't mean fried chicken every Monday night. Four different selections can come from the "possibilities list" each month. This month's menu can later be put in a special envelope to save. It won't be long until there's a regular "menu bank." Then each different menu can be altered to include new ideas, food availability, or special days.

Variety planning helps family members develop the idea of give and take. When manicotti is planned for Tuesday, and Shelley hates it, you can arrange to serve something else that will be her favorite. No, you can't please all the people all the time. But with some variety and spirit we will find at least some time the finicky one is pleased. The purist, too, will be in luck, the one with exotic tastes will be satisfied, and husbands much more content. And best of all—see mother smile.

Why should anyone else treat mealtime like an event—if we don't?

FOURTEEN

THAT'S THE WAY THE COOKIE CRUMBLES

Dear Mom: I've had it! I'm resigning! No matter how hard I try, it seems like nothing ever goes right. I feel like a failure as a wife, as a mother, as anything! It's just not worth it!

There's nothing more realistic in life than facing the fact that there will be times (probably many) that we fall flat on our noses. Spiritually, emotionally, as teachers, wives, mothers, and housekeepers, we will sometimes fail. Just like children, we won't learn the first time. When those moments come, we unfortunately think we are alone. Our pain and disappointment seem unique, and we may conclude that we must be "failures."

We *profess* that pain is a natural part of our journey through life. But we *act* as if disappointments never would have happened if only we had "done a better job." After all, it's the mother's responsibility . . . if our children choose the wrong, it must reflect on us, we think. We have failed.

The truth of the matter is this: The only time *we* have failed is when we never try in the first place. After having fallen flat, we fail if we don't get up and try again. Every failure brings us that much closer to success. But it's just too easy to take temporary setbacks personally; they seem so permanent.

Dust off and pat yourself right on the back. Yes, you get frustrated and fall. But you can also become reinspired and recommitted and try again. Throw your shoulders back and shout into Echo Valley: "I know I'm not perfect. I'm not the model mother, but I'm not the worst by far. As a matter of fact, I'm a pretty good mother. I'm trying hard, and I'm learning."

Every mother deserves at least some self-acceptance. She then can leap forward and give her best in tackling the whole thing over again (and over again, and over again). We sometimes forget that there's a vast difference between a feeling of *humility* and one of *inferiority*. Heavenly Father certainly has confidence in our abilities. Surely he is patient as we diligently work out our winning combinations.

We get disillusioned when we come to grips with facts that are unpleasant. But we were never promised rainbows. Storms will pass through. Things don't always (actually, they seldom) go the way we hoped. Circumstances may disappoint us. Some people may hurt us. And sometimes others simply won't like us or our families. That's really hard to accept (particularly when it involves our children). Would that we could always dwell in the "happy surburbia" of our dreams, but we can't.

Some children were trying to handle their disappointment when someone was cruel to them. Their mother pointed out there were those who didn't like her, either. The children were aghast! Who couldn't like their *mother?* Somehow, we feel that if we are truly living the gospel we will always be accepted warmly. This is not so. And conversely, the fact that we aren't embraced by every associate doesn't necessarily indicate that we aren't living the gospel.

Even the best of us will make bad decisions, and those may throw us off track temporarily. That's no reason to give up the journey, however. Although it may be our plan to reach the destination from Point A by the most direct route, we may get sidetracked. We then may have to take the country roads, but the destination is there still. Yes, reaching it will require more time, but is it impossible? Through a repentant attitude and redirection, that goal is still within reach.

Accept yourself for the good person you really are! Appreciate the efforts of your life as important contributions to eternity, and don't spend your precious time thinking that there's someone out there who is so much better.

As children we always heard the stories of going to grandma's house to find heaps of oatmeal cookies and plates of gooey warm fudge. Whenever friends wore something new they invariably said, "My grandma made it for me." Our grandmother didn't do any of those things. She had a career. But she always brought us doughnuts and candy bars. Every weekend there was a standing date for lemonades at Tunie's. No, she wasn't like everyone else's grandmother. But I always felt sorry for my friends, for I was sure they had been shortchanged in the "grandma department."

Our grandma's house was filled with unusual little things she had gathered throughout her life. Oh, the hours we used them to pretend! We learned to braid hair on her German doll, and we pulled carts and twirled tiny parasols from the Orient. We could bang away on her typewriter to our hearts' content. Her den became our high-rise office, her bedroom our stage, and her yard our African jungle. Her refrigerator was always filled with the good things that got wiped out immediately at home—soft drinks and cookies and peanut brittle. (And we were free to have our fill!) When the family went to her house after a big dinner, we children would immediately head for her refrigerator. It didn't matter that we weren't hungry; food just always tasted better at her house. She never discouraged us from making a mess in her kitchen while cooking date bars, and her extra bed never seemed "extra," for one of us was always welcome to "stay over."

Grandma was like a benevolent dictator. She made sure we saw the error in our ways, but she wasn't ever angry with us. And it never dawned on us that our position with her might have slipped because of the infractions. The word here or the line there have become bits of wisdom that have carried me through some interesting times.

Grandma was our refuge when we were sure that no one in the world cared about us. (Mothers feel they have to set the record straight, but not grandmas. They understand.) When Johnny ran away from school, she found him stomping down the street with determination. But she didn't march him right back. Instead, she took him to get a malt. "It will all come out in the wash," she would say. There wasn't a child in our family who didn't at one time or another announce with finality, "I'm going to live with grandma!" We all knew that to her we were blue-ribbon kids, shining examples of humanity.

Why is this important? Because now in her frail years she questions what difference the simple events of her life have really made to anyone or anything. The beautiful honors that are offered to mothers she probably thinks belong more to someone else—someone who achieved something more significant than raising two daughters and herding a passel of grandchildren. It's difficult for her to appreciate what an impact for good she was in our lives.

Individual worthiness and contribution may be measured by worldly terms in life, but our Heavenly Father sees not as a man, but looks upon the heart. My appreciation for my grandmother transcends the limitations of these earthly generations. There is a mutual acceptance, spirit to spirit, eternal sister to sister.

Keep looking for that silver lining. There's nothing to make a dull day even drearier than being subjected to someone's prophecy of worse to come. We are all familiar with Murphy's Law: Nothing is as easy as it looks, everything takes longer than you expect, and if anything can go wrong, it will—at the worst possible moment. Well, some people make Murphy look like an optimist. We've got to look on the bright side. We might do well to consider the verse:

> When you talk about your troubles
> And you list them o'er and o'er,
> Folks begin to think you like them,
> And proceed to give you more!
>
> (Authorship unknown)

Maria expressed an optimistic attitude in *The Sound of Music* when she mused, "Whenever God closes a door, somewhere he opens a window." The trick is discovering which window he has left open. Perhaps he is trying to see how inventive we can be. The fact that a door is temporarily shut does not mean there's no alternative, however.

Being temporarily stopped may prove to be the real blessing. Analyze a little more closely the saying "stop and think." We do have to *stop* to think. And it could very well be that our most creative periods come during the times we've been "stopped" by our trials. The door may be closed, but creative growth is probably just behind it.

Don't beat yourself senseless. Aren't we all our own worst critics? But if we beat ourselves so unmercifully, we will be too worn out to keep on trying. Heavenly Father has the ability and willingness to both forgive and forget even the most grievous errors. We should be willing to do the same for ourselves. Many nights we thrash about in bed because of some word foolishly uttered or an action unthinkingly made. It doesn't do any good to toss and turn—what's past is past! The important thing is that we have learned from it. Satan surely is pleased as he watches us beating ourselves through guilt and remorse. The Lord's way is that remorse serves to humble us and that we rise above it. We're required to meet and experience trials and sorrow. It's meant that we should overcome them, "for if they never should have bitter they could not know the sweet" (D&C 29:39).

Keep problems in perspective. We make a lot more out of some problems than we really should. Sometimes we think the Lord is truly trying us in the furnace of affliction, when actually, we're only getting a little "singed." It's then that taking a little time for the smoke to clear can help us see things more accurately. In the overall scheme those trials may not be terribly significant, but they surely can knock us off our feet in the present.

Has this ever happened to you? (Of course it has!) You've kept your house immaculate for six months. Then one afternoon you decide to sew and things are a complete disaster. And what happens? (1) Your husband walks in with unexpected company and wants to know if you can "throw together a little lunch," (2)

Your neighbor drops by to introduce herself, or (3) Your visiting teachers pop in for a few minutes.

Having our first baby was certainly an adjustment, as we expected it would be. It didn't really seem difficult, only different. Then the second baby came—things were terrific! The third baby came—everything was still just great! The fourth baby came—my, weren't we having fun, and everything was still basically organized. I remained "in control." But then, in the sixth year, our fifth baby came and the dam burst. Everything seemed to be going to rack and ruin. No matter how desperately I tried, life was just a step ahead of me for a year. I'd pull it together long enough to think that maybe, just *maybe,* the end was in sight. And then, wham—catastrophe! Those five little ones were just like white mice in a cage—constantly churning, exploring, and overturning.

That's when she came—a special lady from the ward—just for a little visit. She met disaster. A few months later she dropped by again, and again she met disaster. I swore to regain total control and that she would never again witness such a state of confusion. Sure enough, the third time came, and things were worse than the first two times. There were two alternatives: (1) I could be reasonable and accept it, or (2) I could become hysterical and rant and moan. I chose the second. Finally, though, reason did come. The experience was over and done with. Self-inflicted misery was not going to change what had happened. She had come, and it was over. There would probably never be anything I could say or do that would alter the opinion she had formed (although I hoped she looked beyond the surface).

These insignificant experiences shouldn't alter our opinion of what we can do. We shouldn't continually live in fear of what others will think, for there are always going to be times that we give them something to think about! We live correct principles for ourselves as well as we can. When the experience is a complete and total flop, accept it at face value, and pick up the pieces. Pat yourself on the back for the times you haven't failed quite so seriously, and then get going again! There's always something or someone to blame for our having "failed." But there is also a means by which we can take control of our destiny and make ourselves into what we should be.

Be realistic in what you expect from yourself. After all, you're only human. Remember, there is a time for every purpose under heaven. Knowing this is one thing, but living it is another.

It seems there have always been, and always will be, basically two types of people: (1) those who do nothing but complain as if they had to do everything, and (2) those who try to do everything as if it were nothing! Neither attitude is the correct one, but if we have to choose between the two evils, let's choose the second. When that shoe does fit, there are people who will try to get you to think that you fit the description popularized by W. C. Fields: "There's a sucker born every minute." In truth, you're probably just trying to serve as best you can.

An older woman said one day, "You young mothers amaze me. You try to do everything. When our children were little my husband wouldn't allow the bishop to call me to any position. My children and home were my Church calling." That attitude is understandable, but it's a good thing everyone doesn't feel that way, or nothing would work. We each have an obligation (and opportunity) to serve where and when we're able. We have covenanted to do so. Service gives us both balance and growth.

However, we need to use our brains. We should analyze our own family's needs and obligations. We can then communicate with Heavenly Father to determine the appropriate extent of our involvement at particular times. Through this verifying process we can stand justified when called to account.

This process, however, calls for our total honesty. What is the real motivation behind our participation (or lack of it)? Is it a sincere desire to serve? Are we fearful of what others will say if we answer no, or do we feel that the bishop will think we're not carrying our load? Do Church callings become a way to "escape" home and family frustrations? Do we decline out of fear of rejection by others who seem "smarter"? Do we feel unqualified, or is that position not "important" enough? Do we accept to serve others or to feed our own egos? Are we overly ambitious? or lazy? *Honest* assessment is the only assessment.

We all need to serve, and Heavenly Father is disappointed when we look for excuses not to do so. But he does not expect one person to carry such a load that she becomes ineffective in the other areas of her life—particularly motherhood.

Solve problems that have caused disappointments, when that's possible. Don't despair—don't pout. Consider the rosy bedtime hour that the books tell about, when children who have cleaned up, washed up, and cheered up sit and share intimate thoughts and beautiful experiences. That should be our opportunity to question, reinforce, and bear testimony. We then tuck them in and they drift off into dreamland. Too bad more children haven't read those books.

We can be thankful that those moments do come sometimes. But there are also other times that seem to have been plucked from a horror story. There may be countless variables at fault: too-tired children, tired or cross mommy, illness, many small children, daddy gone. Pressures come that definitely are not conducive to beautiful moments of solitude. Perhaps the fault is ours, perhaps it is with the children—or perhaps it is merely circumstance. At any rate, the moment doesn't turn out well.

At those times we shouldn't sit dejected in bed and despair of ever "measuring up." Calm down, pray about it, and ask for some guidance in understanding what happened. Pray for direction in solving the problems. Throwing up our arms in despair won't do anything but encourage rationalization when we again find ourselves in the same sad situation. If dinner time was unpleasant and tense, stop and think: Was the meal ready on time? Was there a reason the children were extra hungry? Did you have to threaten them to get them to the table? There are many things over which we have no control, but there are also many situations we can control. Success takes thought.

Try to see some humor in these difficult situations. Although it's not always possible, there are still some seemingly tragic situations that actually could give us a good chuckle if we'd let them. At least humor can help remove that desperate feeling.

A friend and I sent all our children downstairs to play one afternoon, and it wasn't too long before childish howls of delight reached our ears. We went to investigate, fully anticipating some wonderful childhood adventure. (Perhaps they were playing "Primary" or "Happy Family"—or even Robin Hood.) Did we ever have a wrong number! There they were, in the height of their glory, throwing sixty pounds of wheat in every direction. The basement looked like the grain silos of Egypt just before the famine—wheat was everywhere. Like a destroying angel, I stood prepared to mete out justice. But my friend looked at me and cracked a smile. Then she began to chuckle. She had learned to see the humor of the moment.

Little by little we learn the lessons, and it becomes easier. Discipline was necessary, but anger and revenge would not have put the wheat back into the containers. The blessing of seeing the humor is that it tempers the immediate, spontaneous impulse. We can then act, not just react.

Don't be a Jonah. Don't try to hide from the Lord or run away from problems. Accept the Lord's concern for your welfare and realize that he cares about your personal trials. If they are important to you, they are important to him. We need to bear in mind with each crisis in life that we haven't arrived at our ultimate destination.

Life is a journey. The Lord doesn't view us critically if there are valleys as well as upward climbs. The important thing is that as we plot our "average," the curve moves upward. We aren't alone. He pulls us, entices us, encourages us, and many times carries us through our afflictions. As we humbly acknowledge our weaknesses before him, those weaknesses can become our strengths. We're all grateful for the spirits sent to us. We love them, but we need our Father's help in preparing them for their eternal *and* mortal roles. Yes, we will fail, but through it all, we are not alone. We are meant to succeed.

During the times of frustration or resignation, our balance is restored as we consider this message from Elder James E. Faust, a member of the Council of the Twelve: "In the pain, the agony, and the heroic endeavors of life, we pass through the refiner's fire, and the insignificant and the unimportant in our lives can melt away like dross and make our faith bright, intact, and strong. . . . This change comes about through a refining process which often seems cruel and hard. In this way the soul can become like soft clay in the hands of the Master." (*Ensign,* May 1979, p. 53.)

FIFTEEN

THOU ART
AN ELECT LADY

. . . must quickly say good-bye, Mom. A mutiny is about to erupt!

As a mortal woman you have no doubt caught yourself wondering, "Is this really worth it? or "Is this what it's all about . . . I mean, *this* is *it?*" This process is normal and can prove a blessing as we ponder, accept, reach, and change.

We search to find ourselves. The prophet Joseph Smith saw the vision plainly and he emphasized each woman's true status as a daughter of God. The Lord through him told Emma, his wife, "Thou art an elect lady" (D&C 25:3). Each Latter-day Saint woman is, in fact, "an elect lady." Often we become discouraged because of the frailties of the flesh. We worry about ourselves and those placed under our stewardship. Our positions as wives and mothers not only fail to receive many worldly honors, but too many times they do not claim even the respect that should rightfully be found within our gospel family. Trials and obstacles confront us, and we find ourselves tightly tangled somewhere "in-between." We may fail to recognize our true value, not only as wives or mothers or human beings, but more significantly as daughters of our Heavenly Father.

With the birth of our first child (a son! the heir! the name-sake!) my husband and I were so thrilled we thought we had surely died and gone to heaven. But later, with much less fanfare, another little spirit blessed our home. A daughter! And with her came such an outpouring of unexplainable love. We didn't have to die to go to heaven, so to speak, for when she arrived, heaven came with her. Having felt the phenomenon of this gentle stewardship with its special love and protective concern, we have realized all the more what a special place daughters must hold within our Father's heart. From his eternal vantage point our position of womanhood truly is elect.

Mortal man tends to be shortsighted, but inspired man sees the picture clearly. Prophets throughout the dispensations have recognized and reemphasized woman's unique role, her responsibilities, and her refining sensitivities.

Jacob, that stalwart prophet, called men to repentance and reminded them powerfully that their wives and children were exceedingly tender and chaste before God. And it is of particular significance to women, in light of the magnitude of those events transpiring at the time of the resurrection, that it was to Mary that Christ first appeared. To her the awesome privilege was given to bear the glad news: He is risen! It's interesting, too, that it was her welfare that first concerned him. Even before commissioning her with that responsibility, he tenderly inquired, "Woman, why weepest thou?" (John 20:15). He was mindful of her needs, and he comforted her. Yes, our womanhood makes us truly important. We not only carry a heavy responsibility in our Father's plan, but we also fill a place of special concern in his heart.

Occasionally a woman looks about and concludes with bewilderment, "But . . . I'm different." She wonders why, as we each do from time to time: Why can't I be more this way? Why am I not more like so-and-so? Do these differences indicate *flaws?* We were each born with unique abilities and talents, and they are all part of our spiritual personalities. Obviously, there must be a reason for each and every one of them. Each of us is valuable.

There is a unique mission to perform for every different personality and talent.

One sister in our ward teasingly volunteered to help another with an assignment once, and as she did so she laughed, "That's okay, we know you." The one being helped had laughed at herself and was lovingly teased by others because to her one recipe was as good as any other. She made it plain to everyone: Most "Suzy Homemaker stuff" should be spelled *yuck*, and everyone accepted it with a shrug of the shoulders and a well-intentioned laugh. But a different picture came into focus that day. For just a glimpse of a second, there came a look into her eye that said something else. She did seem to care, not about cooking ability but possibly a little about that "different" aspect of her personality.

True, when I looked I didn't see "Suzy Homemaker." What I did see was a warm, caring person with a sparkling personality—an optimist! I saw someone who always sought out others and made them feel at ease, and then built them up. I saw a mother who laughed with her children, and who maintained a tremendous rapport with youth.

In the course of an assignment with the Young Women almost a year after this woman had moved, I conducted a survey. The question was asked, "Who is the woman you would most like to be like, and why?" The majority listed her name. The "why" was answered with variations of "She made me *feel good.*"

The facets of your personality have a place in the pattern and purpose of life. Your special mission in life is to be—*you.* Your special challenge is to return to our Heavenly Father, still you, only magnified! Perhaps the greatest revelation a woman could hope to receive would be for her to catch the true vision of her calling as a handmaiden of the Lord, as a daughter of even God himself! What a blessing it is to fully see what part we play in our Father's plan. We not only set the course, but we determine the outcome of eternities. It is both humbling and spectacular.

Glorified womanhood is truly one of the crowning achievements of all creation. And the reward within our grasp is one of such magnificence that it is presently beyond our means of comprehension. But reach, reach out—it is there. "But as it is written, Eye hath not seen, nor ear heard, neither have entered into the heart of man, the things which God hath prepared for them that love him." (1 Corinthians 2:9.)

P.S. Oh, Mother. I've finally figured it out, I think—why you didn't ever tell me the way things really are or how life would be. I think it was because you knew that never in a million years would I have believed it could be true. (And if I had believed it, that I would have chosen to go through with it.) Thanks, Mom.

INDEX

149

151